A Little

of

Borth-y-Gest

by

Richard Walwyn

**CYFEILLION
BORTH-Y-GEST
FRIENDS**

Many thanks to Aled and Helen Ellis of Minffordd for use of some of the postcard pictures, Chris Mounsey of Sedbergh for the photographs of the haymaking and Garreg Wen Bach and to Robert Dafydd Cadwalader for the painting of the *Fleetwing*.

2nd Impression 2011

ISBN: 978-0-9561469-4-6

Published in 2011 by Delfryn Publications, Delfryn, Borth-y-Gest, Porthmadog, Gwynedd LL49 9TW   Telephone: +44 (0)1766 512115

Cover design by Cathy Woodhead from a tinted print of Moel-y-Gest with Eglwys Ynyscynhaearn in the foreground

Frontispiece from a postcard of Borth-y-Gest c 1890

CONTENTS

Chapter 1 – SETTING THE SCENE

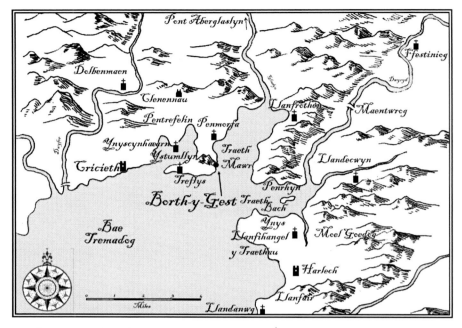

This map is based on one from the early 17th century. Modern spellings have been used and it shows the site of the future village of Borth-y-Gest

Borth-y-Gest may have been so-called because it was the port or harbour of the township of Gest, but it might also have been the entrance or approach to Gest or the ferry of Gest. Gest was a township or *tref* formed almost exactly from the interlocking parishes of Ynyscynhaearn and Treflys.

Walk up to the western summit of Moel-y-Gest (hill of Gest) and you get a raven's eye view of most of the land of Gest. Until quite recently all the flat land you can see from the top of the *moel* was covered by the sea, at least at high water spring tides. The highest tides used to come practically to the bottom of the garden at Wern and the bottom of Penmorfa village in the north, and the large area of low-lying marshy land to the west known as Ystumllyn was flooded by Bae Tremadog (Tremadog Bay) until the third quarter of the eighteenth century, as shown on maps prior to 1780, allowing the highest tides to come practically to present day Pentrefelin.

You can see that Borth-y-Gest is perched on the south eastern edge of what was once almost an island with quite a narrow isthmus. There is an old road joining the two ends of this neck running from the village of Pentrefelin to the entrance to Wern Manor, part of which was once a drovers' road, and which now makes a pleasant walk. In fact before the building of the modern Penamser road in the first half of the 18th century this old road formed part of the only road from southern Llŷn to the east. It is clear therefore that in prehistoric times and right up until the mid 18th century Moel-y-Gest and Borth-y-Gest would have been quite isolated and off the beaten track.

Our corner of Gest is dominated by the *moel* which falls steeply to the old Traeth and Penmorfa marshes in the north, and more gently to the relatively fertile lands of Llannerch y Gest and Tyddyn Llwyn in the south. Nestling under the western end of the *moel* is the ancient house of Bron-y-Foel which was once the major gentry house in our area, though we are surrounded by a number of other once important houses such as Wern, Tu Hwnt i'r Bwlch, Gesail Gyfarch, Ystumllyn, Penamser and Clenennau.

The south western end of the peninsula is the most fertile and is divided into a number of farms such as Tyddyn Adi, Tŷ Mawr, Tyddyn Engan, Glan y Morfa Mawr and others. The cultivated land was never really suitable for anything other than meadow and pasture together with a little poor arable land on which barley and oats were grown for fodder and coarse bread, so the economy of the region was based on the raising of sheep and the local Welsh Black Cattle. The sheep gave wool which was used by a local industry producing flannel cloth.

Some of the cattle used to be sent to market in Shropshire or beyond, and the drovers who took them there over a network of drovers' roads, many of which can still be followed, not only carried on their primary trade but also acted as a vital link between the isolated communities of Llŷn and the much more prosperous midlands of England. They acted as bankers and brought news from England. Some became very prosperous. Having said that, much of the everyday trade to the area would have been by sea. The roads were in a dreadful condition before the building of turnpikes in the early 1800s and much complained about by travellers in the area.

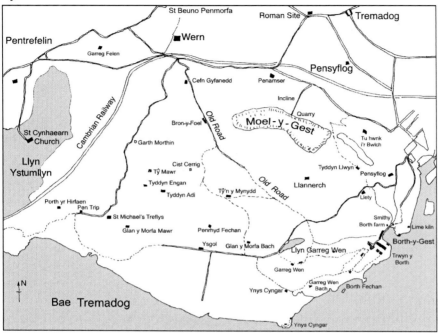

A map showing the area in the vicinity of Borth-y-Gest in about 1870

In ancient times Gest had been a bond township and before 1628 most of Gest was owned by the crown except for the small enclave of Tyddyn y Gest, roughly covering modern Borth-y-Gest. This was part of the Clenennau estate which was inherited by the Ormsby-Gore family of Lord Harlech. It was sold off by auction in 1911.

William Alexander Madocks, the son of the squire of Fron Yw in the old Denbighshire, was born in London in 1774. He was educated in Cambridge, and subsequently became a Member of Parliament representing Boston and Chippenham. On the death of his father in 1798 Madocks was given access to a trust fund which his father had set up on condition it was used for the purchase of land, and this enabled him to buy up much of the land bordering on Traeth Mawr to further his schemes for land reclamation. This included the land where Porthmadog now stands and much of the land surrounding Tyddyn y Gest. The Madocks estate was sold by auction in 1921.

If you had been wishing to travel from Llŷn, say from Cricieth to Harlech at the turn of the eighteenth century you would either have had to go all the way up the estuary of Traeth Mawr as far as Pont Aberglaslyn and then follow the old road through Croesor to Tan y Bwlch, followed by the road that used to run along the high ground via Eglwys Llandecwyn or you would have had to cross the combined estuaries of Traeth Mawr and Traeth Bach to shorten your journey by many miles – perhaps by as much as a day in terms of time.

Before the days of Madocks, the Cob and Porthmadog, the main port on the estuary was at Tŷ Gwyn y Gamlas (the white house by the canal) near the present day village of Ynys on the Meirionnydd side. It was mentioned as such in a jury report of 1650. Tŷ Gwyn had become the port of Harlech after the development of the Morfa Harlech dunes had effectively sealed off the town itself from direct access to the sea.

There used to be a canal connecting Tŷ Gwyn to Harlech, and early maps show an arm of the estuary running behind Ynys almost as far as Harlech. The little port was frequently the subject of romantic paintings, notably by J M W Turner, David Cox and John Varley in the early nineteenth century. Of course, at the time Harlech was the only town of any note at all between Abermaw (Barmouth) and Cricieth (though usually described as "a wretched little village"). One famous ship to be built on the estuary, the *Gomer*, was constructed here in 1821 and was used to transport emigrants from Gwynedd to America, but there are records of ships having been built on Traeth Bach at least as far back as 1772 and probably for a long time before that.

In the 1841 census a man called Edward Timothy, a ferryman, aged between 55 and 60 was listed as living in Plas y Borth, and in 1851 Griffith Jones, aged at least 80, is living at Ynys Cyngar and is recorded as a retired ferryman (in 1841 he is listed as a mariner).

It seems quite likely that there was a ferry which started from Borth-y-Gest and came to the Meirionnydd shore at Clogwyn Melyn on Ynys. There is a road from there which runs via Eglwys Llanfihangel y Traethau to Tŷ Gwyn. The Borth to Clogwyn Melyn passage is about the shortest practicable route across the Traeth (just under two miles). The cottage at Trwyn Penrhyn at the tip of the Portmeirion peninsula is often described as a ferryman's cottage, so that may have been another route. There were other, maybe safer, routes further north than Borth, for example, from Penmorfa or Portreuddyn, and once Porthmadog harbour had been built in 1823 the ferry probably ran mainly from there, but the Borth to Clogwyn Melyn route would have given the shortest journey from Cricieth to Harlech before then.

It is quite easy to row or sail with the flood tide from Borth to Ynys, and then row or sail back on the ebb so, weather permitting, the ferry crossing would not have been too arduous, though it could be dangerous, and on at least one occasion led to loss of life. One also needs to bear in mind that, before the building of the Cob, the volume of water entering and leaving the estuary each tide would have been considerably greater than today, leading to even greater tidal flows than we have now.

Before 1824, when Porthmadog harbour was first used for the purpose, slate was shipped from Ynys Cyngar (Powder House) having first been brought down to wharves on the Dwyryd and then taken by barge for transfer to sea-going vessels moored there. Actually the earliest slate mine in the area, working in the second half of the eighteenth century, was just south west of Bron-y-Foel. Some of the rather poor quality slates from this mine were taken by pack horse or mule for shipment from Ynys Cyngar. The track used for this trade can still be followed.

Those who use the harbour today know it as a splendid shelter from all except easterly gales, which are anyway quite unusual. One can be out in the estuary in a fine old wind but on entering the bay find oneself becalmed − a perfectly splendid harbour, in fact. It may seem odd therefore that at the beginning of the nineteenth century Bae Samson or Samson's Bay in the meagre lea of Ynys Cyngar should have been preferred as an anchorage. We shall see why in due course. During the last few years changes to the level of sand on Garreg Gnwc beach have revealed a line of large stones which may have been associated with some sort of quay on the Borth side of the second Danger Rock – an unlikely anchorage today. Alternatively these may be the remains of an old fish trap.

Of course all the bays would have been used for temporary berths as the numerous iron rings let into the rocks testify.

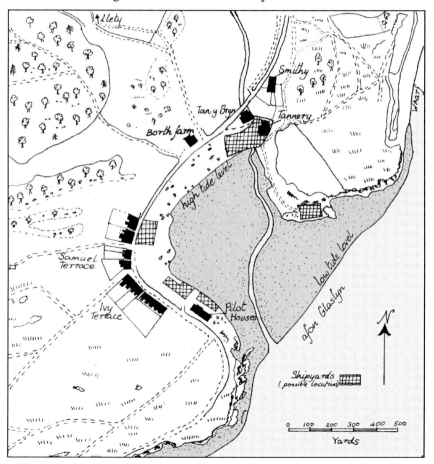

Borth-y-Gest in the early 1860s from a map in Gwynedd Archive

Chapter 2 – PREHISTORY TO ROMAN TIMES

As anyone who has ever tried to garden here knows only too well the village of Borth-y-Gest is built on an area of shaley slate which makes digging a real challenge. This shale was laid down as marine sediment in the Cambrian era more than 500 million years ago. In fact Borth-y-Gest seems to have been at the north western edge of an ancient sea in which, over time, some 15,000 feet of sediment were laid down and eventually heated and compressed to form the rocks we see today. Go down to the beach and you will see the layers sloping up towards the peaks of y Rhinogydd, and in fact this mass of ancient sediment was long ago buckled into an immense mound now known as the Harlech Dome which extends from where we are to Mawddach estuary and includes y Rhinogydd. It was overlain by other rocks in the following Ordovician era, but they and most of the great dome have long been eroded away. Still, while standing on the beach you can imagine that the rocks you see are all that is left of one of the upper layers of this formation.

To the north of Borth the rocks are younger, punctured here and there by the igneous (volcanic) intrusions of dolerite such as Moel-y-Gest and Graig Ddu (Black Rock). The dolerite of Moel-y-Gest was formed by volcanic magma seeping upwards and cooling slowly underground. The covering was eroded to leave behind the more resistant rock. The relatively coarse crystal structure makes these rocks ideal for rock climbers and walkers – they are admirably non-slippery.

Long ago the mountains of Snowdonia were far higher than they are now. As they were eroded over time much of the material would have been ground to silt, but the particle size of more resistant minerals such as quartz remained quite large. This vast quantity of quartz was washed and sorted by wind and water to form the huge deposits of yellow sand we see today and which compose the expanses of Traeth Mawr and Traeth Bach. These sands rely for their purity on a twice daily washing by the fast moving tides. Where the water flow is sluggish, such as in Borth harbour, silts and muds are deposited.

Very much later, quite recently really, our land was covered in ice over a kilometre deep. This gigantic glacier ground down the lower peaks and cut the steep valleys of Snowdonia. As it moved it sometimes tore off great chunks of rock which it carried along, sometimes for great distances. As the ice eventually melted these were deposited to form the so-called erratic boulders we see today, such as Samson's rock and Garreg Wen.

If you climb to the top of Moel-y-Gest you will be able to see the scratches (striations) in the surface of the dolerite made by the overlying ice as it slowly moved by. By examining these you can tell the direction in which the ice was moving – roughly north south. As it ground its way south westward over what was to become Great Britain the ice picked up debris which was eventually deposited as a glacial till composed of boulder clay such as that which forms much of the soil in the area, particularly towards Cricieth.

Actually there is some evidence that some of the deposited material formed a great dam which held back a vast lake of meltwater somewhere to the north. One day that dam was breached and the resulting catastrophic flood spread a layer of debris all over the Llŷn and as far as Graig Ddu or Black Rock. You can still see the remains in the low cliffs to the east of Cricieth.

Sea level has gone up and down over the ages. During the ice age the great weight of ice pushed down on Wales forcing it downwards. As the ice melted this weight was dissipated and the land started to spring back – it is still doing so. If you climb Moel-y-Gest you may be able to make out, about two hundred feet above sea level, the remains of old raised beaches which have now been left high and dry. You may even be able to find shells and sea-smoothed pebbles up there.

The first settled inhabitants seem to have arrived in the area about five thousand years ago. We do not know much about them, but they seem to have been agriculturalists living in small groups mainly on the higher land. At that time the climate was going through a benign warm and dry phase. In our area they left little behind except one spectacular monument known as Cist Gerrig (stone chest), which is shown on maps as Cist Cerrig. This is still impressive, but it is a sad vestige of what it once was. This megalithic tomb (megalithic just means big stone) is on land owned by Tŷ Mawr farm south west of Moel-y-Gest.

Cist Gerrig with Moel-y-Gest behind

Cist Gerrig now consists of three great upright stones arranged in a rough H formation. There would once have been much more, but monuments like this were often robbed to build field walls, and in fact in the later eighteenth and early nineteenth centuries a farmer's lease would often contain a clause stipulating that such stones should be cleared, by gunpowder if necessary. It is really quite surprising how many survive. On a rock face to the south east of Cist Gerrig there is a pattern of small round depressions known as 'cup marks'. Nobody really knows why these were made, but they are thought to be contemporary with the tomb itself. Perhaps they were an early form of art, or they may have had ritual significance. The entrance of the tomb probably faced east, towards the rising sun.

The land round Borth-y-Gest is known as Tre'r Gest (the *Tref* or township of Gest). We do not really know who or what Gest was, but one quite plausible theory holds that this land is named after Cist Gerrig – Cist having been transmuted to Gest. We do know that the name Gest goes back a very long way.

There are other, later, prehistoric remains in the area. Most spectacularly there is the Iron Age hill fort on the western summit of Moel-y-Gest. This is now very ruinous, even more so than when it was recorded by the Royal Commission on Ancient and Historic Monuments in Wales (RCAHMW). They found a fairly extensive system of walls varying from eight to ten feet thick, but they felt it was lacking as a viable defensive structure. It is now proposed that some of these prominent hill forts, and this one is certainly prominent, may have been built primarily for show and as an expression of power and wealth. It would certainly have been an inconvenient place to live, except for the very fit. The nearest water supply is a spring about three hundred feet below the summit, and the best path to the top is pretty steep. By the time this fort was built, about 2500 years ago, the mild dry climate had been replaced by a cold wet one; it is quite exposed on the top of Moel-y-Gest!

The word *moel* means bare hill, and we may assume that Moel-y-Gest, the upper reaches of which are too sparsely covered in soil to support any tree cover, would have stood out as a bare but accessible summit.

The other prehistoric remains are all probably older than the hill fort, but much later than Cist Gerrig. The whole area is littered with the remains of small groups of hut circles, probably dating to the middle to late Bronze Age, a time when the climate was still quite pleasant and good for farming the higher slopes. None of these survive except as rather indistinct markings on the ground.

The Romans had established middle-sized forts at Segontium outside modern Caernarfon and at Tomen y Mur near Trawsfynydd. The road from one to the other possibly followed the path of the modern A487 from Caernarfon to Penmorfa, from where they would have had to cross the two *traethau*. (There was probably another road through Cwm

Pennant and over the mountains to Aberglaslyn, Nantmor, Croesor and Tan y Bwlch which would have avoided the crossing). In any case they certainly came to Penmorfa because they left remains there.

In 1908 a fairly substantial building with a hypocaust (under floor central heating system) was excavated on a site just north of the new bypass roundabout, and during the construction of that roundabout in 2010 another, definitely Roman, site was excavated in a rescue dig. This yielded a quantity of Roman tiles and traces which have been interpreted as the remains of a lime kiln. Local tradition also has it that the Romans mined for iron in the cliffs of Alltwen. It seems likely that the mineral wealth of the area was a major attraction for the Romans. As well as iron there are considerable deposits of lead and copper ore in the area, and even a little gold. However, it seems that the Romans did not actually come to Borth-y-Gest.

Chapter 3 – THE DARK AGES (410AD when the Romans left to 1066)

Borth-y-Gest was, until the building of Porthmadog and even for some time after that, located in the parish of Ynyscynhaearn. St Cynhaearn, was the son of the minor Welsh prince Hygarfael ap Cyndrwyn from Llys Tynwerian in Powys. He lived during the sixth century and that, presumably, is when he founded his little cell on an isolated rocky islet in an inlet of the sea called Ystumllyn. The church now standing on the site, of which more later, was not built until 1832, replacing an older structure. St Cynhaearn's original building would have been tiny.

Another sixth century saint associated with the area was St Cyngar who gave his name to the rocky islet known as Ynys Cyngar on which the Powder House now stands. Prince Cyngar, for so he was, was the son of King Gerren Llyngesog of Dumnonia in south-west England. He was said to have been born around AD 488 but nothing is known of his early life though, as a mature man, he became a follower of his nephew, St Cybi, and may have founded a cell on that suitably remote and inconvenient rock.

The little church of Treflys, perched on the hill top overlooking Morfa Bychan was probably also a very early foundation, though as with so many of the coastal hill-top churches it is dedicated to St Michael.

The land of Gest was in the pre-mediaeval commote of Eifionydd whose *maerdref* or commotal centre was at Dolbenmaen on the crossing of the afon Dwyfor. This was the *llys* or hall of a minor prince. At the beginning of the Middle Ages or earlier the *llys* at Dolbenmaen was fortified. A wooden castle was raised on an artificial mound or motte which still stands in the trees by the roadside, next to the much later Plas Dolbenmaen. Eifionydd and Ardudwy together formed a Hundred or *Cantref* (literally 'hundred townships') called Dunoding, and the prince or minor king of Dunoding would have ruled over Gest.

Then there is the old legend of Cantre'r Gwaelod (the Low Lying Hundred). This is one of the many stories of drowned lands around the coasts of Europe. In this case the land now lost beneath the waves of

Bae Tremadog was supposed to have been drowned in the mists of time when Seithenyn, the drunkard who was meant to be guarding the sluices overdid his debauchery and allowed the tide in. Remarkably there is good evidence that Bae Tremadog was once dry land, but a long time before that. At very low spring tides it is still possible to see the remains of fossilised tree stumps on the beaches north of Abermaw (Barmouth).

The climate during the first millennium AD was cold and wet, and it seems probable that the population density of this part of Wales was very low. We know only too well what happens to land in this area which is not cultivated or grazed – it turns first to scrub with blackthorn, bramble and gorse, and eventually to sessile oak woodland. We may imagine that, before the conquest of Edward I, finalised by the Statute of Rhuddlan in 1284, the land of Gest was largely waste with isolated pockets of cultivation. One ancient farm under Moel y Gest is called Llanerch, which means 'clearing', and was possibly a clearing in the scrub. The standard of living was very poor indeed compared to the far wealthier people of England; indeed it remained so well into the middle of the nineteenth century.

To add to the backwardness of our corner of Gest we must remember that until Madocks built the Cob in 1811 it was composed of a peninsula almost completely isolated from the hinterland. At high tide the sea came right round the north side of Moel-y-Gest as far as Penmorfa, the low lands of Morfa Bychan were underwater and on the far side of Graig Ddu the 'lake' of Ystumllyn reached right up to Pentrefelin, leaving only a narrow neck of land joining Moel-y-Gest to the rest of Eifionydd.

This isolated and barren place where the soil was poor and thin was farmed where possible by tenants bound to their landlords by ties amounting to slavery. They were not free to move from place to place and owed duties of labour to their lord. In short, the land of Gest was a 'bond' township.

Chapter 4 – THE MEDIAEVAL PERIOD (1066 to 1485 and the accession of Henry VII)

On the morning of 9th April 1188 Giraldus Cambrensis (Gerallt Gymro or Gerald of Wales) set off on horseback from Llanfair just south of present day Harlech where he had spent the night in order to ride to Nefyn on the north coast of Llŷn. He was going to spend the night there. His party had spent the previous night in Tywyn, Meirionnydd, crossing the Mawddach and Artro rivers to get to Llanfair. But this day's journey was to be quite a marathon. He was accompanying Baldwin, Archbishop of Canterbury, on a journey through Wales in order to drum up recruits for the Third Crusade, and in due course would write an account of their progress. Of course they had to cross both Traeth Bach and Traeth Mawr. Luckily, as the moon was just three days past the first quarter, the tides that day were neap and low tide was about midday. So long as they didn't mind getting their toes a bit wet and had a good guide, they should have been able to ride across.

We do not know their exact route, but they would certainly have started off over the high ground from Llanfair in the direction of Eglwys Llandecwyn, riding along the ancient track which one can still follow and passing below Moel Goedog before coming down to Traeth Bach, either through Eisingrug or Soar. They seem to have missed Harlech altogether – of course the castle as we know it today would not be built for another hundred years.

From the Meirionnydd shore of Traeth Bach the most direct route to Nefyn would have taken them via Penrhyn, then Borth-y-Gest, Penmorfa and Llangybi. In any case they crossed without incident, having been welcomed into his domain by the local prince Maredudd ap Cynan.

This Maredudd owned Tre'r Gest but, nearly a hundred years later, Edward I conquered Wales and took possession of those lands which had previously been in the hands of the Welsh princes. At this time Gest became crown land, and its lowlier inhabitants remained as unfree as they had been before the conquest. After the conquest the crown does not seem to have taken much interest in its newly acquired lands.

The Welsh gentry, called the *uchelwyr*, established many of the farms we know today.

In the absence of a royal presence there was much encroachment on crown land including, as it happens, that small patch of land which came to be known as Tyddyn y Borth, or Borth farm.

During the ensuing centuries, at least up to the time of the Civil War, the *uchelwyr* entertained themselves by studying their pedigrees – always a matter of immense concern in this part of the world – fighting each other and increasing the size of their estates. This last they did either by carefully arranged marriages, simple theft, protracted lawsuits or, as a last resort, by purchase.

The rising of Owain Glyndŵr at the beginning of the fifteenth century was brutally put down and was followed by one and a half centuries of depopulation and, apparently, misery. How much these tumultuous goings on affected the tenants of Tyddyn y Borth we do not know, but they must surely have been aware and concerned about the great happenings over the water in Harlech Castle where Owain held court in 1404 and which finally fell in 1409.

While all this was going on at home in Wales, the Hundred Years War was being fought on the continent, and our local *uchelwyr* were involved in that. On the south western slopes of Moel-y-Gest there is an old house called Bron-y-Foel. This may, in earlier times, have been the *llys* or court of the minor princes of Gest. In the middle ages it became one of the major 'gentry' houses in Gest.

Just above the house is the spring which supplies it with water, and of course most of the more isolated houses would have been sited close to springs, though until the beginning of the nineteenth century Bron-y-Foel would hardly have been isolated, standing as it did on one of the main thoroughfares in the area. In fact the track on which it stands was the only road into the Borth-y-Gest peninsula until the end of the eighteenth century.

There are many stories associated with this house. In the 14th century it was the home of Hywel ap Gryffydd or Hywel Y Fwyell (Howel of the Battleaxe). The bard Iolo Goch wrote a poem about Hywel in 1380 called, rather verbosely:

"A cywydd to Sir Hywel y Fwyall when he was made a knight in France by Prince Edward, the son of Edward III, when the King of France was captured. It was a popular belief among the Welsh that the King was indeed captured by Sir Hywel, resulting in a gift of a joint of meat by the King for himself and another for his famous axe, plus the revenues from the Caerleon mills and Criccieth Castle and its associates."

The poem (a *cywydd* is a type of alliterative Welsh poem) tells how Hywel, fighting at the battle of Poitiers in 1356, and using his axe managed to chop off the head of the French King John's horse, taking its rider prisoner. The result was a decisive Plantagenet victory. France was asked to pay a ransom equivalent to twice the country's yearly income to have the King returned. John was permitted to return to France to try to raise the required funds. Following some time in France, John subsequently handed himself back to the English, claiming to be unable to pay the ransom, and he died a few months later.

Hywel was rewarded by Edward III with a knighthood and he was also given the rents of the King's mills on the afon Dyfrdwy (river Dee). In addition he was also given permission by the Black Prince to build a mill at Aberdywarch, the village now called Pentrefelin (mill village). In about 1376 he was made Constable of Cricieth Castle, and towards the end of his life he received a pension from the King. Sadly the story of Hywel capturing the French king is probably apocryphal, but he did fight at Poitiers and probably at Crecy as well. Also his exploits with his axe clearly made an impression because it is said that the Black Prince gave the weapon a place of honour in the royal hall, ordering food to be served before it daily, which was later distributed as alms, a practice that continued until the reign of Elizabeth. In 1359 he became constable of Cricieth Castle where he lived until his death in 1381.

Clenennau, built in 1550, was another house which, though not in the immediate area, would have been of considerable importance to the tenants of Tyddyn y Gest. It was the home of their landlords.

Chapter 5 – THE SEVENTEENTH CENTURY

Most of this chapter concerns people and events only indirectly connected with Borth, but which had an impact on ownership and future events. With the Tudors and Stuarts we move into an era where there is far more written evidence than before. In particular Sir John Wynn of Gwydir near Llanrwst wrote his family history in the early years of the seventeenth century – the manuscript is in Cardiff.

The Wynns of Gwydir belonged to a family which had spent the 14th and 15th centuries in consolidating small estates in the townships of Penyfed and Pennant in Eifionydd. At some point they also managed to appropriate part of the township of Gest. About the beginning of the 14th century, Dafydd ap Gruffydd of Nantconwy (claiming descent from Owain Gwynedd) married Eva, daughter and heiress of Gruffydd Fychan, one of the coheirs of 'Gwely Wyrion Gruffydd' in Penyfed. Their descendants came to own most of the gentry houses in the area, including Gesail Gyfarch, Ystumcegid, Clenennau, and Bryncir.

During the revolt of Owain Glyndŵr, Ieuan ap Maredudd ap Hywel ap Dafydd ap Gruffydd of Cefn-y-fan (later called Ystumcegid) and Gesail Gyfarch supported the crown and died in 1403 while defending Caernarfon Castle against Glyndŵr's forces; his brother, Robert, was one of Glyndŵr's followers and received a pardon from Henry, prince of Wales, in 1408. As a result of this division of loyalties, the bulk of the family possessions remained in the possession of the line of Ieuan ap Maredudd until 1463; in that year, the lands were partitioned and Gesail Gyfarch fell to the share of Ieuan ap Robert ap Maredudd (1437-1468). He was a Lancastrian and died of the plague at Gesail Gyfarch in 1468. His son, Maredudd, saying that he preferred to fight the notorious bandits infesting the countryside round Dolwyddelan rather than be murdered by his close relatives, took a lease on the castle in about 1489; he later built Penamnen, and finally purchased Gwydir from Dafydd ap Hywel Coetmor about 1500.

The branch of the family remaining at Clenennau in Eifionydd eventually produced the remarkable Sir John Owen, about whom more will be said soon.

Sir John Wynn who lived from 1553 to 1627, writes in his family history:

You are to understand that in Evioneth there were two sects or kindred, the one lineally descended of Owain Gwynedd, prince of Wales, consisting then and now of four houses, viz., Keselgyfarch, y Llys ynghefn y fann, now called Ystymkegid, Clenenny, and Brynkir, Glasfryn or Cwmstradllyn; the other sect descended of Collwyn [ap Tangno], wherof are five houses or more, viz. Whelog, Berkin, Bron-y-foel, Gwynfryn, Talhenbont, and the house of Hugh Gwyn ap John Wynne ap William, called Pennardd, all descended of their common ancestor, Ievan ap Einion ap Griffith.

Sir William Maurice (1542 – 1622), the eldest son of Moris ap Elis of Clenennau, was a contemporary of Sir John Wynn. Luckily we have a good deal of the correspondence between Wynn and Maurice who, during interesting times, were respectively High Sheriff and Deputy Lieutenant of Caernarfonshire. In particular they were jointly responsible for raising troops and supplies in preparation for the impending invasion by the Spanish Armada in 1588.

Sir William was a member of an old Caernarfonshire family, which in the course of the previous century had accumulated the most extensive and compact freehold estate in south Caernarfonshire, and which centred on the manor house of Clenennau and extended into Anglesey and Meirionnydd. Sir William's father who had been the first of the family to adopt the English form of surname, spent much of his life in the effort to extend and consolidate this estate, a task involving him in constant litigation and frequent turbulence. Sir William's first wife was Margaret Wyn Lacon of Porkington (Brogyntyn) near Oswestry. Through her the Clenennau family estate was extended further into England.

(The patronymic naming system of the Welsh whereby a son took his father's Christian name as a surname, possibly preceded by 'ap' was retained in the poorer classes until well into the nineteenth century, but the gentry began using the English system of family names from the fifteenth century onward.)

When he died Sir William was buried in Eglwys Penmorfa and succeeded at Clenennau by his grand daughter Elin (born 1578), the daughter of his eldest son William Wyn Maurice who had died in 1568. Elin was the widow of Sir Francis Walsingham's secretary, John Owen of Bodsilin on Anglesey, and when she died in 1626 the estate passed to her son Sir John Owen, born in 1600.

Sir John Owen is one of the most colourful characters in the area during the seventeenth century. Very briefly, he was born at Clenennau in 1600 and inherited the estate in 1626, but his early adult life is obscure. By the time he appeared on the scene the glory days of his great grandfather Sir William Maurice were over and though the Clenennau estates were large they seem not to have yielded a huge income. Sir John was first and foremost a soldier. He may have had military experience early in life, but he shot to prominence during the Civil War as one of the staunchest supporters of Charles I. He was sheriff of Caernarfonshire in 1630-31 and of Meirionnydd next year, and when the Civil War broke out he was put on the commission of afray for Caernarfonshire and given the job by Charles of raising and equipping from county funds a regiment from the three shires of Gwynedd.

His neighbours put up objections – they would have to pay after all – and he was not able to put his recruits into the field until the following summer, first in operations round Oxford in 1643, then at the siege of Bristol where, while in command of the 6th brigade under Rupert he was wounded in the face. He wrote home saying that a bullet had passed in to one cheek and out on the other side, but he recovered. He came home to Clenennau in 1644 and was reappointed as sheriff of Caernarfonshire, remaining in office until the king's authority there ceased.

After the successful invasion of Wales by Sir Thomas Myddelton he was summoned to Oxford, where the king made him governor of what became the 'frontier garrison' of Conwy, and a week later, a knight.

He spent 1645 seeing off threats to Sir Ddinbych (Denbighshire) and Sir Y Fflint (Flintshire) and then returned to attend to the defences of Gwynedd. Supplies were sparse and the local gentry slow to co-operate, partly from that fear of alien military rule and occupation. They found a spokesman in Archbishop John Williams who was defending his native Conwy as a depot and objected to the rough-hewn Owen muscling in, but in May Owen forcibly entered the castle, appropriating its contents, and denounced the archbishop in terms which drew a rebuke from the king himself.

Owen held out in Conwy Castle until November 1646, when he surrendered with honourable terms enabling him to retire to Clenennau after taking the Covenant. A fortnight before this, Rupert had written from France inviting Owen to bring over a Welsh brigade for the French service, an invitation he reluctantly declined for lack of means of transport. In the second Civil War his commission was renewed, and he raised Meirionnydd for the king. He led the siege of Caernarfon but was forced to retreat through Bangor before superior forces, with the wounded parliamentary sheriff, William Lloyd, as his prisoner. He was trapped on the seashore at Llandygai, where his men were scattered by Mytton and he himself captured. His prisoner the sheriff died of the rigours of the journey. Owen was committed to Denbigh Castle, then brought to London for trial on charges of treason to Parliament, violation of his articles of surrender, and murder of the sheriff.

He was removed to Windsor and brought for trial after the Lords had resolved, two days after the king's execution, to try him with the chief instigators of the second Civil War. After a spirited defence without the aid of counsel, he was condemned to death. On being told that he was to be beheaded he thanked the court, saying that he was honoured to be treated to that death rather than being hanged as a common criminal. This speech must have made an impression because he was reprieved, though various interventions on his behalf probably helped. By July he was free to entertain John Evelyn in London with a Welsh harpist, and he was home in September. He was charged with a huge fine of £771 which Clenennau could not raise, but he was forgiven.

Owen now lived absorbed in dogs and hawks at Clenennau, forbidden to travel without a pass, and three times put under preventive restraint. He remained a thorn in the side of Parliament during the Interregnum but took little active part in sedition. On the king's return he petitioned for redress for his wrongs, and was given the vice-admiralty of North Wales, and spent some time rounding up the fallen faction in Caernarfonshire, turning the tables on some his old enemies. He died at Clenennau in 1666 and was buried in Eglwys Penmorfa in a vast tomb which local tradition maintains also contains the body of his horse. Some accounts maintain that this is actually the tomb of his grandfather, Maurice.

Sir John's ancestors had accumulated a considerable and learned library at Clenennau; Sir John added one book – on firearms.

Sir John's younger brother William (1607-1670) also fought on the Royalist side in the Civil War, and it was William who inherited the Shropshire Brogyntyn Estate but died without an heir, so the two estates were reunited under Sir John's son William Owen (1624-1677). He married into the Anwyl family of Parc.

William's son Sir Robert Owen (1658-1698) further extended the family's territory in Wales by marrying Margaret the heiress of Glyn Cywarch near Talsarnau. He was knighted for political services, but spent most of his time on the Brogyntyn Estate maintaining close contacts with North Wales. A succession of English marriages, issuing in the devolution of the estate on the Anglo-Irish family of Ormsby-Gore, failed to break this connection, the family alternately representing Welsh and Salop constituencies in Parliament, until in 1876 it entered the peerage with the territorial title of Harlech.

During the first half of the seventeenth century the crown needed to raise funds urgently and did so partly by selling off crown land. In 1628 the bulk of the township of Gest was sold to the Mayor and Commonalty of the City of London, presumably as an 'investment opportunity' because in 1632 they sold it on to Charles Jones from whom it was inherited in 1679 by Colonel William Price of Rhiwlas.

In passing we should mention Richard Edwards (1628-1704) of Nanhoron on the Llŷn. He was a highly competent lawyer and a convinced Puritan who had been active during the Interregnum and on the Restoration was naturally thrown into gaol in Caernarfon. However his largely Royalist clientele of local squires petitioned successfully to have him released so that they could carry on with their consuming passion for litigation over land. Richard Edwards had an encyclopaedic knowledge of Llŷn genealogy on the finer points of which such disputes tended to hinge.

It so happens that the record of one of these lawsuits survives from 1682. Richard Price of Rhiwlas, who had recently inherited much of Gest, set about trying to clear from his newly acquired lands those who had encroached on crown property over the years. The ensuing enquiry called as witnesses all and sundry, including Richard Edwards, who could testify how long all the various interlopers had been in possession. One of the disputed properties was "Tyddyn-y-Borth and Ferry", perhaps the first written evidence that a ferry used to ply from Borth to the Meirionnydd side of the traeth. Tyddyn-y-Borth was claimed by Sir Robert Owen of Clenennau, and the inquiry seems to have concluded that his family had been in possession of the holding from time immemorial, so he kept this small enclave in the surrounding ex-crown land.

However, despite this small failure the Price family managed to establish their claim to the bulk of Gest. They were absentee landlords though they did maintain a foothold in the form of the Elizabethan house called Garreg Felen near Pentrefelin where they came from time to time. Their importance to Borth-y-Gest lies in the fact that the Prices eventually came to own all the land surrounding Tyddyn y Borth, and it was from them that William Alexander Madocks bought much of the land he accumulated towards the end of the eighteenth century.

A view undreamt of before the nineteenth century

Chapter 6 – THE EIGHTEENTH CENTURY

Whereas the seventeenth century had been an altogether exciting time for Borth-y-Gest – quite a lot too exciting at times – the eighteenth turned out to be rather dull. The two main landlords lived far away, the descendants of Sir John Owen of Clenennau, owners of Borth farm, lived at Brogyntyn in Shropshire. The Prices who owned the surrounding lands lived at Rhiwlas near Bala. The old mansion of Clenennau declined into ruin and was replaced by a new, much smaller, farmhouse farmed by tenants. Garreg Felen was maintained by stewards, as was Glyn.

It appears that the absentee landlords took little interest in their Caernarfonshire lands, leaving their administration to bailiffs and stewards. Travellers to the area found the scenery 'horrid' and 'bleak', the roads such as they were 'appalling' and the natives 'incomprehensible and backward'. Actually the 'natives' seem to have been not altogether unhappy with this state of affairs.

The century was a period of dramatic agricultural progress elsewhere in Britain, but our corner seems to have muddled on in the old ways. In fact it seems to have been an age of increasing poverty.

We have one piece of documentary evidence from the middle of the century which throws some light on the quality of life enjoyed by the tenants of Tyddyn y Borth. In 1747 William John Evan, the tenant, died intestate. The procedure in such circumstances was for a bond to be taken out under the auspices of the ecclesiastical court of Bangor so that the deceased's possessions could be assessed and passed on. For this to happen at all there needed to be some property involved – most people in the dioceses left too little to make the business worthwhile.

In this case the petition for administration is made by Anne, his widow, and John Williams the dead man's son (note the patronymic). Both sign the bond, but Anne was obviously illiterate so makes her mark (a circle), while John signs in a very shaky hand. Two assessors are appointed whose job it is to set out an inventory of the dead man's possessions, which in due course they do.

The list makes for quite dispiriting reading:

A True and perfect Inventory of all and singular Goods, Cattle and Chattels of William John Evan of Borth-y-Gest in the parish of Yniskenhaiarn in the County of Carnarvon yeoman lately Deceased and was appraised by the Subscribers as underneath this 27th day of April in the year of our Lord 1747-

Item	*Three cows and Calfs valued*	*6:5:0*
Item	*Six Ewes and Lambs valued 3:6*	*1:1:0*
Item	*Six Sheep more at 3:0*	*0:18:0*
Item	*The Household Stuff Valued in all*	*12:00:0*
Item	*Tools of Husbandry Valued*	*00:12:0*
Item	*Five Goats and four kids Valued*	*00:16:8*
		21:13:8
	Arrears unpaid to William Owen	*4:0:0*

Richard David/Thomas Rowland

So, William Evan left £17–13–8 to his widow, equivalent to about £1500 in today's money. That was not much from a relatively large farmer.

That is not quite the end of the story because we know that the tenant of Borth farm, a holding of just over 129 acres, in 1750 was Dafydd Humphreys in whose family it stayed until after 1790.

Plas y Borth was the home in the mid 18th century of a certain Captain Williams who was reputed to be a smuggler. The story goes that he ran a friendly house where people would gather for a Noson Lawen or merry evening – a pub in all but name in fact. After one of these the young harpist Dafydd y Garreg Wen is said to have made his unsteady way home via Garreg Wen rock on the hill above Tan y Foel, where he lay down to sleep things off. He woke in the morning to hear a lark ascending above him, and was thus inspired to write the tune *The Rising of the Lark*.

Being a smuggler was not an occupation confined to the criminal classes of Llŷn. Many everyday articles such as coal and salt were heavily taxed in the eighteenth century and the local gentry were not above taking action to avoid paying what they regarded as iniquitous taxes.

Right at the end of the eighteenth century the area woke up to find that a human dynamo had descended on them in the form of William Alexander Madocks. The story of how Madocks transformed the fortunes of our corner of Caernarfonshire has been told many times elsewhere, and it is not proposed to go over it all again. Much the best account is given in '*Madocks & the Wonder of Wales*' by Elisabeth Beazley.

We should just note that from 1798 Madocks started buying up the land he needed to carry out his schemes for reclaiming land from Traeth Mawr, and eventually most of the Price holdings came into his possession. But the effect on Borth-y-Gest of those developments will take us to the next chapter.

Ferries from Borth-y-Gest to Harlech would have landed near here.
From a painting by John Varley of Tŷ Gwyn y Gamlas in c 1805

The County Archive in Caernarfon has a copy of the advertisement for sale by auction on 18th September 1797 of the estates of the late Richard Tavistock Price in the Township of Gest, in the Parish of Ynuscynhayarn in the County of Carnarvon. Richard Price was the illegitimate son of the previous owner of the estate. He borrowed heavily, mainly through mortgaging parts of the estate. He was not to enjoy his inheritance for long, as he died at the age of thirty-nine years in 1794, leaving his encumbered estate in trust for his thirteen year old son, Richard Watkin Price. This sale was presumably intended to redeem some of the mortgages. The properties offered for sale, not all of which were knocked down, included [spelling as used at the time] Gareg Felen, Bron y gader and Mill, Glan y Morfa bach, Garreg Wen, Llanerch y Gest, Tyddyn llwyn, Pen y clogwyn, Ty whynt yr Bwlch, Llidiart y Sputty with Ynusfadog cottage, Tan'r allt ucha and Cwm Mawr. A contemporary pencilled note states that Penyclogwyn was sold along with Ynys Tywyn.

William Alexander Madocks bought Tan yr Allt and Penyclogwyn at this sale. He presumably acquired some of the other properties later, perhaps by private negotiation with the estate.

The sale particulars list how much land the tenants were obliged to drain, the yearly rents due to both landlord and crown and a number of other conditions they had to meet including planting "Gorse and quicksets in the hedge rows, and to blast and remove unnecessary stones". That presumably explains what happened to many of the area's antiquities.

Right at the beginning of the nineteenth century in 1801 Bron-y-Foel came under the hammer. The sale particulars in this case are much less formal than the major sale of the Price holdings, but make interesting reading and are here reproduced in full:

Caernarvonshire

To be sold by Auction at the King's Head in Carnarvon on the afternoon of Saturday the twenty first Day of February 1801 Subject to certain Conditions then to be produced unless previously disposed by private contract of which the Public would be duly apprized.

An extremely eligible and compact Farm called Bron-y-Foel situate in the Parish of Treflys and now let to Humphrey Humphreys as tenant from year to year at a very easy Rent, it consists of such arable meadow and Pasture Land, is for the most part bounded with a thorn hedge, has an uncontrolled Right of Common on Morfa Bychan and lies within a Mile of the Market Town of Penmorfa and a smaller Distance from the High Road leading from thence to the Towns of Crichieth and Pwllheli: There is upon this Farm a Slate Quarry the Profits whereof might be extended to a great Degree if carried on with proper spirit as its situation is not only very convenient for Home Consumption but it lies extremely Advantageous for Exportation being close to a Harbour called Ynys Cyngar which Admits of Vessels of 200 Tons Burthen.

The Tenant will shew the Premises and further Particulars may be had by applying to Messers Cook Horney at Carnarvon.

The claim concerning the slate quarry was, perhaps, an early example of Estate Agent's hyperbole. In fact this was an underground mine rather than a quarry, and the quality of the slate produced was very poor, being badly contaminated with sulphur which caused it to delaminate in a short time. For all that, we are told that much of Tremadog was originally roofed from this mine. It also seems doubtful that 200 ton ships could really have used Ynys Cyngar anchorage – it never became a proper harbour, though Madocks did have ideas to build one there before building of the Cob led to the formation of Porthmadog.

Chapter 7 – THE NINETEENTH CENTURY: Regular census returns

The reader has probably noticed that Borth-y-Gest does not seem to have featured much so far. The reason for that is simple; it hardly existed before about 1850. A visitor to Borth in, say, 1810 would have found a silted up harbour possibly filled with quite high dunes like those behind Black Rock sands today. Inland from these dunes would have been a small farm – Tyddyn y Borth – and further round, where the Pilot Houses now stand, would have been the crumbling remains of an old house called Plas y Borth. No more. If our visitor had climbed the dunes he would have been able to look across the salt marsh to Trwyn Penrhyn a mile away and he would have been able to make out the Glaslyn river in the distance flowing past that point.

A walk along the low cliffs towards Cricieth would have taken you past Borth Fechan, Garreg Wen Bach and Garreg Wen farm before dropping down to the salt marshes of Morfa Bychan. Looking out towards Harlech you might have seen one or two small sailing vessels loading and discharging cargo under the lea of a rocky island called Ynys Cyngar, and at the foot of the cliffs you would have found a row of single storey one or two roomed cottages also known locally as Ynys Cyngar. They still exist but have been transformed into one dwelling.

Heading back to Borth and setting off in the other direction towards where Porthmadog stands today you would have climbed the hill and found, at the top, the little farm called Penyclogwyn – it is still there – but beyond that you would have found your way blocked by salt marsh again. You might have tried the path behind Borth farm, in which case you would have come to the two cottages known as Llety, and beyond them the small holdings, *tyddynnod*, of Llannerch and Llwyn. Again, no more.

What changed all this was, of course, the building of the Cob in 1811. Once that was complete the Glaslyn, instead of flowing a mile away, was forced into a new channel right past our harbour. The harbour remained full of sand at least until 1840, but sometime soon after that it must have been cleared.

The map Madocks used in his bid to get an Act of Parliament giving him harbour rights in 1820 says that Borth harbour is "an old harbour now filled with sand" while a map of 1775 drawn up during an early proposal to dam Traeth Mawr shows the Glaslyn running close under Penrhyn and nowhere near Borth.

In 1838 an Act of Parliament was passed to commute the tithes paid to the vicar by all farmers and tenants from a contribution in kind to a money payment. (Anybody who held land had to pay tithes until quite recently.) The act called for a comprehensive survey of all landholdings, as a consequence of which a map was produced together with a schedule listing all parcels of land with their owners, tenants, field names, areas and what they were used for. The act did not insist on the drawing of a new map so that the one used may have been an old one. As it shows just the beginnings of Porthmadog it probably dates from between 1820 and 1830. It shows Borth harbour as dry land, called Traeth it is true, but listed as sand and waste in the tenancy of Borth farm, the property of Ormsby-Gore.

Apart from Plas y Borth all the houses just mentioned still stand, though much transformed and 'improved'. Penyclogwyn farm and Llety are the least altered, but the rest have been enlarged and pebble-dashed out of all recognition.

There is one 'house' standing in the modern village which still bears a passing resemblance to an early nineteenth century residence. Have a look one day at the garage behind N° 2 Bron Afon. In fact it is not a garage at all, though it has been used as a workshop until recently. Hidden behind the modern boundary wall is what was clearly a cottage with a central door and a twelve pane sash window on either side. It is a single storey structure, but its surprising height probably indicates that it once had a *croglofft* – a sleeping balcony at the end furthest from the road. At the road end there is a substantial chimney. Actually this little building is very solidly constructed and may actually be contemporary with the main house, but it could be a lot older. Old records refer to a house called Borth Uchaf (upper Borth) which is hard to identify; maybe this is it, though there are other candidates.

From 1841 onwards the ten-yearly census records form a valuable source of historical information. The census actually started in 1801, but the earlier ones are not nearly as useful as those from 1841 onwards because they only have overall totals and no details of individual households, the original enumeration sheets having been lost. The census was carried out by an enumerator who first distributed census forms then, after census night he would walk round the village collecting the forms which he would transcribe onto enumeration sheets. It seems that the order of entries on these sheets more or less corresponds to the route taken by the enumerator. The country was divided up into 'Enumeration Districts', and Borth came under Ffestiniog. This can prove problematic since it leads to Borth being included in Meirionnydd. Enumeration districts were subdivided into parishes – ours being Ynyscynhaearn – and later into villages. For each household individuals present on the night are listed by name together with their age, sex, marital status, occupation and relationship to the head of the household. Later on their place of birth and language spoken were also recorded, together with whether they were deaf or blind.

Identifying houses in the returns can be quite tricky. The street names changed over time and the modern system of house numbering was only introduced in the 1891 census. Before that houses in a street were numbered, if at all, in the order the census enumerator came to them as he walked round the village.

Samuel cottages almost certainly turned into Seaview Terrace, and Borth Road became Mersey Street, but some remain obscure – Borth Uchaf for example. The only really satisfactory way to settle the identity of a house is to compare inhabitants from one census to another, and there seems to have been a lot of population movement. One particular problem concerns the Pilot Houses; now there are four, but it seems there may once have been as many as seven.

In 1841, as has been said already, Borth consisted of about five houses. Plas y Borth houses a pilot and a ferryman and a mariner lives in the cottages at Ynys Cyngar. Otherwise the main occupation is farming.

Borth's attention seems to have been turned inland. This is borne out by the book called 'Y Gestiana'. Robert Isaac Jones of the Pill Depot in Tremadog who wrote it was born in 1815, and was therefore well aware from personal experience of the condition of Borth in the 1830s and 1840s – he has little to say about it and that only in terms of its farming connections.

By 1851 there are more signs of maritime activity. Llety, which was then two cottages, is in the hands of a ship's carpenter and there is another living at Ynys Cyngar. A ship loader lives at Borth Fechan who might have worked in Porthmadog or perhaps at the vanished quay below the house. Richard Jones of Garreg Wen farm who later became a noted shipbuilder is still listed as a farmer and has not yet given up much of his land in favour of a new trade. Plas y Borth on the harbour seems to have been replaced by seven houses all lived in by pilots. However these houses are not yet named, being referred to simply as Borth N°1, Borth N°2 etc. There are references to two more houses which I have failed to identify. One was obviously quite large as it housed a Proprietor of Houses, his brother who was a Curate, his two sisters – an Attorney's Wife and a Merchant's wife, three children and a servant. In the other lived a ship's carpenter with his wife and four children together with his brother who was also a ship's carpenter and a servant.

Of course the absence of mariners in all the censuses is partly to be explained by the fact that only those actually present on the night of the enumeration are counted and mariners were often away at sea, but their wives are still shown as mariners' wives, and those there seem to be concentrated more in Morfa Bychan than in Borth. One entry for the rather unhelpfully named Tai Newyddion N°2 (New houses number 2) which appears to have been in Morfa Bychan shows up one of the pitfalls awaiting census readers. The Householder, Evan Roberts, is a stonemason while his 18 year old mariner son is called Robert Evans. This is one of many examples of the patronymic naming system whereby a son took his father's Christian name as a surname. Anyway, the picture that emerges in 1851 is of a small settlement of Pilots in Borth proper, a few surrounding farms and a growing but rather poverty-stricken settlement in Morfa Bychan.

By 1861 there is quite a little settlement of five dwellings around Ynys Cyngar where at least three seamen live. Garreg Wen is still being farmed on quite a large scale (200 acres) but Garreg Wen Bach now houses a ship's carpenter, his wife and seven children. Borth Fechan has an agricultural labourer's widow living alone, but the big development is round the harbour. The Pilot Houses are now known as Henblas Terrace (Old Plas Terrace) and of the seven houses four are occupied by Pilots. The others house a slate quarryman, a stone cutter's labourer and a merchant seaman's wife (possibly widowed).

Pilots in the pilot launch at the end of the 19th century

There are two major new developments though; Ivy Terrace (ten houses as today of which two remain unoccupied) and Samuel cottages consisting of five houses which are probably the first five houses in the modern Seaview Terrace. Of course this implies that both were built between 1851 and 1861.

In Ivy Terrace there are three Pilots, a ship's carpenter and four Master Mariners. In Samuel cottages there are a Grocer, two Master Mariners, a Master Mariner's widow and a ship's carpenter. In addition to Borth farm and Llety, of the two houses known as Borth Uchaf one is occupied by a Ship Builder and the other by a Dock Labourer; they may have been the first two houses in what became Glyn Terrace, but the 1865 development plan of the village does not show any building there at all. Also we now have the first mention of a smithy housing a Blacksmith and a yard housing a Ship Builder.

Clearly between 1851 and 1861 Borth has started to develop as a maritime community housing, on the whole, high status people such as master mariners and pilots. Also there are now signs that shipbuilding is becoming established. Presumably the harbour has now been cleared or dredged. We know that the pilot launch was originally kept in a purpose-built dock which had been blasted out of the slate below the modern house called Merionfa. In this way it was close to the river, but not very well sheltered.

Between 1861 and 1871 there was a major housing boom. By 1871 Bron y Garth has been built and is the property of Charles Spooner the civil engineer of the railway, Craig y Don is established as a shipyard – the first house there was probably not built until 1884. The Smithy and Borth farm continue as before, but we now have the first mention of a public house, The Gest Inn under the landlord Robert Richards from Ffestiniog which is now 9 Seaview Terrace. Samuel cottages have turned into Samuel Terrace and have expanded from five to eight houses (nine if you include the Gest Inn) and we now have two grocers. Amanda Terrace features for the first time housing pilots and mariners; the two Bron Afon have just been built, one at least being a Lodging House.

The decade from 1861 to 1871 was also notable for the arrival of the mainline Cambrian Coast Railway at Porthmadog in 1867. This led to the gradual decline in shipbuilding as the slate output of the Ffestiniog mines was transferred from sea to rail. It also led to the final cutting off from the sea of Ystumllyn, because the railway to Cricieth was built along the top of the shingle bank between the lake and the sea which was stabilised for the purpose. This was also the era of the rise of the British seaside resort, and the railway meant that it was now relatively easy for people to come from the Midlands and the north for holidays.

The Ormsby-Gores realised Borth's potential as a holiday destination and, perhaps in anticipation of the arrival of the railway, commissioned a number of proposals for the more lucrative development of their property. Much of the Harlech Estate archive has been deposited at the National Library of Wales in Aberystwyth, and this includes two such proposals, neither of which was actually constructed.

The first plan, which can be dated to 1865-66, would have seen a convex marine crescent of eighteen houses occupying the land now taken by Bron Afon, St Cyngar's Church and Garreg Llam. It was proposed to build a school roughly where Glyn Terrace is now; an existing well is shown opposite the north end of Ralph Street where the first five houses at the southern end of the harbour side are already under construction. It was proposed to have a chapel at the north end of Glyn Terrace (which was not yet named), and another road parallel to and west of Ralph Street (to be called Gore Street). There would also have been a sizeable hotel at the northern end of this road roughly where the house called Achipur now stands.

On this plan Ivy Terrace and the Pilot Houses, together with the first seven houses of Seaview Terrace are shown complete; 8 Seaview Terrace and the houses on the south side of Mersey Street between Ralph Street and the harbour are shown under construction.

The second plan which dates from a year or two after the first, perhaps 1867 because Bethel is shown under construction, shows the harbour side of Ralph Street nearly complete with work beginning on the other side as well. Amanda Terrace is under construction. Plans for a school seem to have been abandoned in favour of Glyn Terrace which is under construction. The big terrace on the front has also been abandoned, though the road round Carreg Llam is still called Marine Terrace; Bron

Afon is under construction and so is most of the south side of Mersey Street, Bethel and Wesley chapels and the north side of Mersey Street (still called Borth Road). The proposal for a Gore Street and Hotel is still alive, but no more than a proposal. Other proposals were for a reservoir roughly at the top of Tan y Foel, and for five large detached villas on the land now occupied by St Enodoc, Wendon, Ysgol Borth-y-Gest and the Parc y Borth reserve. Once again, none of these proposals were ever put into effect, but it is chastening to realise that the idea of Borth as primarily a holiday resort is nearly 150 years old.

The Pilot Houses at the time of the 1871 census are a bit of a mystery. They may be the six houses referred to as Borth-y-Gest Road, but if so they are no longer lived in by Pilots except one; all the rest have moved over the road to Amanda and Ivy Terraces. Instead the inhabitants are labourers and common sailors (as opposed to master mariners). Perhaps at this time the Pilot Houses were being built or falling into decay. Altogether there are eight pilots living in Borth at this time, three in Amanda Terrace, three in Ivy Terrace, one in Glyn Terrace and one in Borth Road.

Three major developments have taken place between 1861 and 1871. Nearly all Mersey Street has been built, including Capel Bethel which is dated 1867; all Glyn Terrace has been built and a considerable part of Ralph Street – all the houses on the harbour side and some on the other as well. Altogether this represents a huge increase. Borth-y-Gest has been transformed from a tiny hamlet into a substantial village within the space of ten years.

The land on which all these houses were built belonged to the Ormsby-Gore (Harlech) Estate, and if N° 2 Ralph Street which was built in 1866 is representative of the rest, which seems likely, they were erected on 66 year building leases at a nominal ground rent of £1, the estate retaining the freehold until the great sale of 1911 when nearly all the houses in Borth were sold to their tenants.

A couple of other things are worthy of note; Richard Jones of Garreg Wen farm has reduced his acreage from 200 to 50, and we know that he was now concentrating his energies on shipbuilding, and a Dutch sailor,

Leendert Van der Velden has married a Welsh girl and is living at Ynys Cyngar.

A large proportion of the population is described as having something to do with the sea – they are master mariners, sailors, shipbuilders or labourers in the docks. There is a fair smattering of tradesmen such as joiners, shoemakers, quarrymen and so on, but Borth-y-Gest has clearly turned its face away from the land and out to sea.

Between 1871 and 1881 the pace of development slowed. Seaview Terrace was extended as far as Ebenezer (dated 1880); the Gest Inn, though still so called, is now lived in by a slate quarryman rather than a publican; the first five houses of the modern Seaview Terrace are still known as Samuel cottages or Terrace in 1881. Ivy Terrace is unchanged from ten years before, as is Amanda Terrace. The Pilot Houses are now known as Pilots' Terrace for the first time; there are seven of them, but three are now unoccupied. Both Bron Afon houses are unoccupied. Mersey Street is probably unchanged, though confusingly the top part, above Glyn Terrace, has reverted to being called Borth Road. Glyn Terrace itself is unchanged. From the census return it is possible to follow the route taken by the enumerator and in this case it seems he climbed the bottom part of Mersey Street, walked down Glyn Terrace and back, crossed over to the north side of Ralph Street and back along the south side and then turned left up the top half of Mersey Street. The 1865 Harlech Estate plan calls Mersey Street Borth Road, so perhaps this was still the name above Glyn Terrace, or perhaps the enumerator simply had a lapse of memory.

By 1891 there have been some fairly minor developments; we now have a tannery – probably where Min y Môr stands now. The Gest Inn has a publican again, though he also works as a stevedore. Rather splendidly there is a dwelling called Ogof y Gwalch (rogue or hawk's cave) which seems to have been between the Tannery and the newly built Glan Eifion. The name Samuel cottages has finally disappeared and Seaview Terrace is complete. There are now five Pilot Houses (two pilots and three mariners). Mersey Street is complete. Ysgol Borth-y-Gest was founded in 1880 and the school house first appears in 1891. On the west side of Ralph Street N°s 1 to 9 and 17 to 23 have been built leaving gaps to be filled later. Otherwise little has changed.

In 1901, once again little has changed. The number of Pilot Houses has come down from five to the present day four; in Ralph Street N°s 11 and 13 are being built but are not yet complete. The Tannery is now called The Yard and Ogof y Gwalch is no longer mentioned.

This brief description of the census data barely scratches the surface. In many ways the most interesting things they tell us concern the lives of Borth's residents; their jobs, family relationships and inter-relationships, the number of children they had and so on. Here we have the makings of a book! As a taster Appendix A traces one family living in one house from 1841 to 1901, and Appendix B traces another extended family which included three pilots.

Borth-y-Gest at the turn of the century

Chapter 8 – THE TWENTIETH CENTURY: Estates sold off

There were major developments in the twentieth century, mainly in the 1930s and 1960s. The interwar years saw a considerable amount of building on the Garth on the north side of the harbour together with extensions past the school and the big houses between the school and the sea.

The modern development of Tan y Foel began with the demolition of 13 Seaview Terrace and the beginnings of a road over the hill to Morfa Bychan planned by Graham Bourne, thankfully never completed. Earlier in the century there was a certain amount of infill building round the bay, and the black and white houses on Borth Road seem to have been built about 1909. Many residents have clear childhood memories of the village during the 1930s, 1940s and 1950s. There was more intensive grazing in those days, so there was much less bracken and scrub. There were large bell tents for hire on the beaches during the summer months and many will remember the Beach café at the end of the beach path.

Tents for hire in the early 1900s

The Harlech Estate disposed of all its land in Eifionydd (over 3000 acres) by means of a series of auction sales in 1911. The catalogue of the Borth-y-Gest sale includes interesting maps, and many extant copies have been annotated with the prices reached. The following table is taken from one such catalogue; note that in some cases a number of houses were sold as one lot, so the price realised needs to be divided accordingly.

Lot	No	Street	Sold as	Modern Name	Price (£)
140			Pen Rhiew	Penrhiw	130
141			Bryn y Parc	Bryn Parc	430
142			Parc y Borth	Parc y Borth	300
143			Building Plot		200
144			Tan y Bryn	Tan y Bryn	345
145			Building Site	Glanaber Garage	50
146			Parc-y-Borth House	Borth farm, Borth dairy, Borth Wen	380
147			Building Site	Village field by Parc y Borth	Given free
148			Building Site	Nature reserve by Parc y Borth	500
149			Building Site	Tan y Foel Estate	
150a				Layby on Seaview Terrace	
150			Plot by Ebenezer	Tŷ Aber Borth	
151				Bus shelter plot	
152				Car park	
153	1	Pilot Houses		Plas y Borth	
153	2	Pilot Houses		St Agnes	
153	3	Pilot Houses		Plas Môr	
153	4	Pilot Houses		Min Afon	
154				Carreg Llam	
155				Carreg Llam	
156				Carreg Llam	

Lot	No	Street	Sold as	Modern Name	Price (£)
157				Twr y Gwynt	
158				In Glyn Terrace by Bethel	
159	30	Mersey Street	Building Plot	Vacant space for 30 Mersey St	
160			Borth Fechan	Borth Fechan	Withdrawn
161	1	Bronafon		Bron Afon 1	170
162	2	Bronafon		Bron Afon 2	172
163	1	Amanda Terrace		Eryldon	100
164	2	Amanda Terrace		Bron Glaslyn	50
165	3	Amanda Terrace	Gwynant	Henryd	80
166	4	Amanda Terrace	Cartref	Cartref	85
167	5	Amanda Terrace	Cwyredd	Gwynedd	82
168	6	Amanda Terrace		Amanda	83
169	7	Amanda Terrace	Min y Don	Min y Don	100
170	1	Ivy Terrace		Ivy Cottage	60
171	2	Ivy Terrace		Awel-y-Môr	60
172	3	Ivy Terrace		Lantern Cottage	60
173	4	Ivy Terrace		Moorings Bistro (Mrs Tibbs)	Withdrawn
174	5	Ivy Terrace			51
175	6	Ivy Terrace		Gwynlys	Withdrawn
175	7	Ivy Terrace			Withdrawn
176	8	Ivy Terrace			62
177	9	Ivy Terrace		Adref o'r Diwedd	62
178	10	Ivy Terrace		Bron Allt	71
179	1	Seaview Terrace		Dolphin Cottage	130
179	2	Seaview Terrace		Drws Nesa	130
180	3	Seaview Terrace			136
180	4	Seaview Terrace		Seaview Tearooms	136
181	5	Seaview Terrace		Bay Stores	70
182	6	Seaview Terrace	Glanavon	Glanafon	100

Lot	No	Street	Sold as	Modern Name	Price (£)
183	7	Seaview Terrace		Glan-y-Don	100
184	8	Seaview Terrace	Maelgwyn	Maelgwyn	97-50
185	9	Seaview Terrace	Gwynfa	Gwynfa	97
186	10	Seaview Terrace	Llwyn Dewi		65
187	11	Seaview Terrace	Llys Llewellyn	Llys Llewelyn	65
188	12	Seaview Terrace	Glaslyn	Ardwyn	65
189	13	Seaview Terrace		Demolished	64
190	14	Seaview Terrace		Was Bobbing Boats	60
191	15	Seaview Terrace	Glandŵr	Glandŵr	60
192			Isallt	Isallt	70
193			Glan Eifion	Glan Eifion	70
194			Isfryn	Alderly	65
195			Islwyn	Islwyn	65
196			Lluest	Gwenelgon	Withdrawn
197			Glanaber	Glanaber	Withdrawn
198			Smithy & Garden	Gwynant Cottage 1 & 2	Withdrawn
199	1	Ralph Street	Brynawel	Brynawel	85
200	3	Ralph Street	Llys Dewi	Llys Dewi	60
201	5	Ralph Street	Talafon	Talafon	62
202	7	Ralph Street		Bryn Derfel	Withdrawn
203	9	Ralph Street	Arosfa	Morfa	60
204	11	Ralph Street	Bryn Môr	Bryn Môr	30
205	13	Ralph Street	Morawell	Morannedd	33
206	15	Ralph Street	Velog	Velog	36
207	17	Ralph Street			Withdrawn
208	19	Ralph Street	Trigfan	Trigfan	44
209	21	Ralph Street	Hyfrydle	Hyfrydle	44
210	23	Ralph Street	Faith	Faith	44
211	25	Ralph Street	Rhianfa	Rhianfa	
212	27	Ralph Street	Tawelfa		
213	29	Ralph Street	Gwynfa		

Lot	No	Street	Sold as	Modern Name	Price (£)
214	31	Ralph Street	Albert House	Albert House	
215	33	Ralph Street	Arfryn	Arfryn	
216	35	Ralph Street	Frondeg	Frondeg	
217	37	Ralph Street	Gwenallt	Gwenallt	
218	2	Ralph Street	Trem y Don	Trem y Don	82
219	4	Ralph Street		Bodwyn	67
220	6	Ralph Street	Preswylfa		67
221	8	Ralph Street		Gwyddfan	62
222	10	Ralph Street		Pennant	67
223	12	Ralph Street		Wen Llys	67
224	14	Ralph Street		Avondale	65
225	16	Ralph Street			67
226	18	Ralph Street	Idea House	Gellifor	60
227	20	Ralph Street	Berwyn	Berwyn	60
228	22	Ralph Street	Bodaufor	Bronwydd	60
229	24	Ralph Street			60
230	26	Ralph Street		Llys Beuno	30
231	28	Ralph Street		Bryntirion	60
232	30	Ralph Street		Gowerian	60
233	32	Ralph Street	Alltwen		60
234	34	Ralph Street		Maweni	80
235	36	Ralph Street	Angorfa	Angorfa	60
236	38	Ralph Street	Hafod	Hafod	60
237	1	Mersey Street	Post Office	Post Office	90
238	2	Mersey Street		Arosfa	40
239	4	Mersey Street			40
240	6	Mersey Street		Trem yr Hafan	40
241	8	Mersey Street			40
242	10	Mersey Street			40
243	12	Mersey Street		Malindi	40
244	3	Mersey Street		Is-y-Bryn	40

Lot	No	Street	Sold as	Modern Name	Price (£)
245	5	Mersey Street		Heulwen	40
246	7	Mersey Street			40
247	9	Mersey Street			45
248	11	Mersey Street			45
249	13	Mersey Street		Tŷ Chandos	50
250	14	Mersey Street		Terfyn	50
251	15	Mersey Street		Noddfa	
252	16	Mersey Street		Foelas	35
253	17	Mersey Street		Melangell	40
254	18	Mersey Street		Bryn Goleu	40
255	19	Mersey Street	Maenllwyd	Maenllwyd	40
256	20	Mersey Street			
257	21	Mersey Street		Ger y Coed	
258	22	Mersey Street	Ael y Bryn		16
259	23	Mersey Street	Fro Fair		16
260	24	Mersey Street	West Ari	West Aria	16
261	25	Mersey Street	Bryn Hyfryd	Bryn Hyfryd	40
262	28	Mersey Street	Pen Rallt	Pen Rallt	
263	29	Mersey Street	Rand Hill	Bron Yna	29
264	1	Glyn Terrace			30
265	2	Glyn Terrace	Gowerian	Glyn Cottage	
266	4	Glyn Terrace			
267	5	Glyn Terrace		Erwydwen	
267	6	Glyn Terrace			
268	8	Glyn Terrace			
269	9	Glyn Terrace			55
269	10	Glyn Terrace			55
270	11	Glyn Terrace		Llanor	
270	12	Glyn Terrace			
271	13	Glyn Terrace		Glascoed	
272			Borth y Gest School	Ysgol Borth y Gest	

Much of what is now Parc y Borth nature reserve was offered for sale as building plots.

Haymaking in 1940 in the white rock (Garreg Wen) field

In January 1921 the Tremadog Estate was also sold by auction, so those properties which stood on what had originally been land owned by the Price family of Rhiwlas now came up for sale. Of course the Tremadog Estate covered a much larger area than Borth-y-Gest, so the following table is only partial. It is interesting to notice, by the way, that Borth Fechan was offered as part of the Harlech estate, while Borth Fechan cottage (Fuchsia Cottage) next door came up with the Tremadog sale. The old boundary wall between Tyddyn y Borth (Clenennau land) and the crown possessions in Gest runs between the two.

Lot	Description	Price (£)	Tennant	Sold to
1	Llannerch y Gest	WD	Mr John Humphreys	
2	Tyddyn Llwyn farm	1050	Mr Wm Griffith Morris	
3	Tu-Hwnt-ir-Bwlch	1000	Mr Richard Davies	
5	Pen-y-Clogwyn farm	1000	Mr John Edmunds	W D Griffith

Lot	Description	Price (£)	Tennant	Sold to
6	Lletty or Lletty'r Celyn	650	Mrs A Humphreys	D Breese
7	Garreg Wen farm	1320	Mr H T Hughes	R Newell
7a	Garreg Wen lake	80		D Breese
8	The Golf Links	650	Mr H T Hughes	Chivers
10	Garreg Wen Bach farm	575	Mr Evan Jones	
14	Tŷ'n-y-Mynydd cottage	60	Mr Hugh Jones	Tenant
15	Hendy or Tŷ'n-yr-Ardd	80	Mr Griffith Williams	Tenant
16	Siloam cottage	120	Mr Robert Buckley	Tenant
17	Pen-y-Llyn cottage	60	Mr H W Humphreys	
18	Moelfre cottage	100	Mr Thomas Humphreys	
19	Borthfechan cottage	155	Mr Ellis Humphreys	
22	Pen-y-Clogwyn Isaf Fields	275	Mr Edward Griffith	J Davies
24	Land near Bron-y-Garth	500	Mr Casson	Mr Casson
25	Field near Craig-y-Don	140	Mr John Roberts	
26	Penamser farm	750	Mr Hugh Jones	Tenant
27	Pensyflog farm	2500	Mr Henry Roberts	

Peaceful scene c1900 with Bron Afon and Marine Terrace

Chapter 9 – THE SHIPBUILDERS

We tend to think of Borth-y-Gest as a shipbuilding harbour, and for a relatively brief period so it was. In fact it really began to develop as a village in the 1840s when the original pilot, John James, who had been recorded living in Plas y Borth in 1841 was joined by six more. Their job was to guide ships in and out of the new Porthmadog harbour. Appendix 4 at the end of this booklet tells the awful story of the day when four of the pilots were drowned in one terrible accident.

Emrys Hughes in *'Porthmadog Ships'* records 35 ships being built in Borth harbour between 1845 and 1880 – an average of one a year during that period. The majority, 18 ships, were built by William Griffith between 1846 and 1872; Richard Jones of Garreg Wen built five (possibly six) between 1873 and 1878; Simon Jones built two or three between 1863 and 1876 and various other people are recorded as building one ship each. Obviously building a ship was not a one man job, and Emrys Hughes points out that the recorded builder was not always the actual man in charge of the job. In addition, William Hughes is recorded as building three ships in Porthmadog and Simon Jones five in Porthmadog.

William Griffith, aged 30, is recorded as living at Borth N° 9 in 1851 with his wife Jane of the same age, their four children, William's brother and a servant. In 1861 they have moved to Borth Uchaf and now have seven children and are in Glyn Terrace in 1871 and 1881. By 1891 Jane Griffith is a widow, living in 4 Glyn Terrace. By 1901 Jane has died and William's son Griffith Griffiths who is also a ship's carpenter is living in the same house with his sister Jane (49) and his brother Owen (40) also a ship's carpenter.

Richard Jones was living at Garreg Wen farm in 1841 aged 24. He has not yet married his wife Mary, but is recorded as a farmer and the head of a household of nine souls, some of whom will have been farm workers or indoor servants. At that time Garreg Wen farm extended to about 50 acres. By 1851 Richard has married and has a 10 month old daughter Ellen; the farm has extended to 200 acres and there are now four male and two female servants living there. In 1861 he is still farming 200 acres, but now with only two men and one inside servant. 1871 sees the farm reduced to 50 acres and now there is only one male and one female servant living in. It is at this point that he starts building ships. By 1881 Mary has died and Richard, still described as a farmer, is living with Ellen and her husband Richard Vaughn (also Jones) together with their young children Richard Vaughn and Mary Jones. In 1891 Richard Jones senior, now 75, is still a farmer and head of the household; Richard Vaughan Jones is now described as a ship's carpenter and, aged 47, shares the house with his growing family.

When trying to identify particular shipyards it is necessary to bear in mind that the building of a wooden ship was a very much simpler business than the term 'shipyard' might convey. In the eighteenth century and earlier, ships were built all along the Welsh coast and along the sides of the estuaries including Traeth Bach and Traeth Mawr, sometimes on exposed beaches. A builder would select a likely spot, lay down some sort of standing and then get on with the job. Eventually, when it came to launching time some means would have to be found of floating the vessel, but this could well have involved dragging and levering the ship on the highest of spring tides.

Quite a few large vessels were actually built a surprising distance from the water. The result is that we should not necessarily expect to see permanent 'slipways'. Rather we would be likely to find places where a particular builder was in the habit of working. Also some facilities may have been shared. We know, because it is marked on early OS maps, that there used to be a sawpit in the middle of the modern car park. All ship builders would have needed access to a saw pit – they were dealing with large baulks of timber – but they did not necessarily need one each.

William Griffith apparently built at least some of his ships where Craig y Don now stands. Richard Jones's 'yard' was by the modern Min y Môr, and there were at least two other 'yards'; Simon Jones usually built where the car park is now and under Tai Pilots (or Pilot Houses). Emrys Hughes only listed the major sea-going ships which regularly took on cargo at Porthmadog and there would have been plenty of other boat-building work going on, enough perhaps to occupy the eleven locations shown on at least one plan of the harbour.

Borth produced many fine ships; notable for its size was the 402 ton *Snowdonia* built under Tai Pilots in 1874 by Morris Owen. He may have been the widowed master mariner living at 1 Amanda Terrace in 1881. Morris Owen employed a certain John Hughes to design this ship and supervise her construction. She was lost with all hands near Holy Island while laden with phosphate rock after only seven years in 1881.

Another big ship was the 206 ton *Fleetwing*, built by Richard Jones in 1874. She led an eventful life and was still in existence as a coal hulk in the Falklands during the war of 1982.

A painting of the Fleetwing by Robert Dafydd Cadwalader

I have a particular interest in the *Sarah Evans*, a little 98 ton two masted topsail schooner which was built by Richard Jones in 1877. The previous owner of my house, Captain Robert Roberts, sailed in her as an Ordinary Seaman in 1900 at the age of 12. The ship was owned by his father, Captain Evan W Roberts, and in 1907 Robert Roberts took over command at the age of 19. Robert Roberts did not then have his deep sea ticket, so an older certificated sailor, William Ellis, went with him. The *Sarah Evans* plied her trade mostly round the coasts of England and Wales, with the occasional trip to Ireland or the Continent. She was sold away from Porthmadog and eventually wrecked off Lands End in 1932.

Below is a list of the ships built in Borth-y-Gest according to *Porthmadog Ships* by Aled Eames.

Name	Built	Builder	Tons	Master	Lost	Notes
Lara	1844		106	J Roberts		
Jane Catherine	1845	Robert Owen	78	Griffith Williams	1872	Lost with register off Portland
Daniel Morris (1)	1846	Wm Griffith	83	R Parry	1855	
Martha James	1847	Wm Griffith	99	John Ellis	1874	
John Williams	1848	Wm Griffith	74	John Thomas	1895	
Louisa	1849	Wm Griffith	59	John Thomas	1895	Lost off Bishop's Rock
Martha Gertrude	1851	Wm Griffith	53	Thos Jones	1872	Lost with all hands
Mary Lloyd 1	1852	Isaac Lloyd	63	Isaac Lloyd Morris	1893	
Charlotte	1852	Wm Griffith				
Marion	1853	Wm Griffith	67	Wm Roberts	1885	Lost off Cricieth loaded with lime
Sydney Jones	1856	Wm Griffith	80	Morris Jones	1869	
Elisabeth and Ellen	1857	Wm Griffith	81	J Thomas	1892	Built under Craig y Don

Name	Built	Builder	Tons	Master	Lost	Notes
Daniel Morris (2)	1858	Wm Griffith	98	E Roberts		
Elizabeth Richards	1858	Wm Griffith	66	Wm Roberts	1879	Lost with All hands in Sligo Bay
Nathaniel	1858	Wm Griffith	98	John Jones	1878	Sold to pay for divorce
Ann Griffith	1859	Wm Griffith	107		1866	Lost off Copenshay
Alert	1860		46		1876	Lost off Ireland
Ardudwy	1863	Richard Jones	203	Wm Williams	1869	
Volunteer	1863	Wm Griffith	116	Evan Jones	1903	Lost on Goodwins
Edward Windus	1864	Wm Griffith	156	E Williams	1904	
Minerva	1866				1870	
Wave (2)	1868	Wm Griffith	149	Ellis	1881	
Pride of Wales	1870	Simon Jones	288	David Morris	1893	
William Jones	1870	Wm Griffith	79	W Evans		Lost near Dungeness
G and W Jones	1872	Wm Griffith	103	Griffith Jones	1888	
Carl and Louise	1873	Richard Jones	144	John Roberts	1877	Lost with all hands
Fleetwing	1874	Richard Jones	226	Owen Jones		Last survivor now broken up
Snowdonia	1874	Morris Owen	402	Capt J Roberts	1881	
Blanche Currie	1875	Richard Jones	193	David Evans	1914	Named after sister of Williams of Castell Deudraeth

Name	Built	Builder	Tons	Master	Lost	Notes
Criccieth Castle	1876	Simon Jones	218	John Morris	1882	
Edward	1876	Richard Jones	140	J Ellis	1892	Master drowned with ship
Ida	1877	David Jones	179		1890	
Sarah Evans	1877	Richard Jones	98	E W Roberts	1932	
Cadwalader Jones	1878	John Hughes	103	John Cadwalader	1933	
Dizzie Dunlop	1878	Richard Jones	99	T E Williams		Last master Owen Humphreys ran navigation school in Borth
Thomas Owen	1880	John Williams	71	Tom Williams	1890	

A fishing smack in the bay in 1890s. Craig y Don boatyard is on the right

APPENDICES

Appendix A: GARREG WEN BACH – Sixty years of one family

Garreg Wen Bach, now modernised and extended, was from 1841 at least until 1901 a smallholding lived in and farmed by one extended family whose story can be traced through the census records. When I first knew the house it had fallen into picturesque ruin. We have at least two paintings of it made in the mid twentieth century showing it unencumbered by the trees which surround it today. The family history is complicated and there are one or two uncertainties.

In the 1841 census ages were recorded to the next lowest multiple of five years, so someone who was actually 84 years old was recorded as being 80. In 1841 the head of our family is listed as Rice Samuel, aged 80+ and described as a farmer, who is living with his wife Catharine Samuel aged 70+, their daughter Elin Samuel aged 50+ and their grandson-in-law William Williams aged 20+ who is described as a carpenter. His wife Sarah does not appear in the record for another twenty years, but would have been about fifteen in 1841. Perhaps William was a lodger who fell in love with the visiting granddaughter of the master of the house.

By 1851 Rice (Rhys?) has died and the widowed Catherine, aged 83, is the head of the family but appears to have changed her name from Samuel to Williams; her daughter, now called Ellen Pierce (an example of the patronymic system) is 63 and still unmarried. Also living with them are the two children of William and Sarah, Jane aged three and Catherine aged two. William and Sarah are not recorded.

In 1861 Ellen (now spelt Ellin) Pierce is living alone in part of the house, while William Williams (45), now a ship's carpenter and his wife Sarah (35) are living in the rest. They now have seven children. Jane (15) and Catherine (13) have been joined by William (11), Pierce (9), Ellin (7), Eliza (4) and Sarah (2). These ages do not quite tally with those given ten years earlier, but that is not uncommon.

In 1871 the now elderly Ellen Price (another name change) is said to be living in the stable and described as a housekeeper. William (56) and Sarah (48) have the main house. William is still a ship's carpenter, and also living in the house are their son William, now 21 and a carpenter and two new children, Thomas (9) and Lewes (7). The other children are not recorded so either they were away from home that day or they are working away from home.

By 1881 Ellen has died so William (66) and Sarah (58) share the house with their four unmarried children Jane (32) – a waitress, Elizabeth (25) – a dressmaker, Sarah (21) – a housemaid and Thomas (19) who is a joiner.

Garreg Wen Bach in the 1940s with Ynys Cyngar and Samson's Bay

William has died by 1891 and the widowed Sarah, presumably aged about 68 though recorded as 77 is the head of the household. Her daughter Jane, still single, is living with her and her daughter Catherine has married a mariner from Bardsey Island, Evan Jones, and they are also living in the house together with their son William Jones (6) and Sarah's granddaughter Ellen P Williams aged nine. This last Ellen must be the child of one of Sarah's boys.

Finally, in 1901, Evan Jones has come ashore and is now described as a labourer in a shipyard. His mother in law the widowed Sarah Williams (77), his wife Catherine, their son William (16) who is now a sailmaker's apprentice and their niece Ellen are all living together in the same house that, perhaps, Sarah was born in 77 years earlier. She is, at any rate, described as having been born in the parish of Ynyscynhaearn.

Appendix B: THE MORRISES – a family of pilots

If the story of Garreg Wen Bach was the story of a house, this is the story of a mainly seafaring family among whom were three pilots.

In 1851 Evan Morris aged 47 is living at a house referred to as Borth N° 3 with his wife Jane (42) and his five children Griffith (20), Ellen (13), Ann (7), Evan (5) and David who is 2. Evan senior is described as a Pilot whilst his son Griffith is a Moulder. This could either mean that he is a foundry worker or a shipwright.

In 1861 the family has moved to the newly built 4 Ivy Terrace. Evan (still a pilot) is 58 and Jane is 53. Griffith and Ellen have left home; Griffith seems to have moved away from Borth altogether and so has Ellen unless, of course, she has married and acquired a new name. Ann, Evan and David are still at home and a visitor, William Lewis, is also staying in the house on the night of the census. Evan junior is a 15 year old mariner.

By 1871 Jane has died so Evan senior is listed as a widower aged 67 and is still working as a pilot. His unmarried daughter Ann, now 26 years old, is looking after him but Evan junior has set up house in 5 Glyn Terrace and is now a pilot like his father. 'Young' Evan has a wife called Jane like his mother, and they have two children – Jane (2) and John (5 months). They also have an eleven year old girl, Ann Ellen Griffith, living with them as a servant. Evan's brother David is not registered – he would be 22 and is probably away at sea.

In 1881 Evan senior does not appear, so we must presume he has died. Ann also has left the record, so she has probably moved away as she does not seem to be living in Borth as a 36 year old wife. 'Young' Evan, now aged 34 and still working as a pilot has moved from Glyn Terrace to a house described as N° 5 Pilots' Terrace – a puzzle as there are now only four Pilot Houses. However, in 1881 there are seven Pilot Houses listed. He has with him his wife Jane, and they now have five children, Jane (12), John (10), Evan (8) Ann (5) and Griffith (4). In 1880 Evan had been involved in a ghastly accident when he was the only survivor out of four Borth pilots when their boat had been overpowered by strong seas on the Bar. There is a newspaper account of this tragedy in Appendix 4 to this book.

Evan's brother David (32) is a mariner and has settled in Mersey Street – probably N° 4 – with his wife Ellen, also aged 32 and their two children

Eliza (6) and David junior (2). They actually have another daughter called Ellen who is four, but she seems to have been away from home on census night.

In 1891 'Young' Evan's daughter Jane, now 22 years old, is married to a 30 year old mariner called John Watkins and they are living in N° 1 Seaview Terrace. They have yet to start a family.

'Young' Evan is now 44 and still living in one of the Pilot Houses – perhaps the same one as there now appear to be five of them and he seems to be at one end or other of the row. Jane, John and Evan have left home, but their places have been taken by Mary (8), Hannah (6), Emily (3) and Robert (1) – nine children altogether.

Also in 1891 David is still at N° 4 Mersey Street, but he is now also a Trinity Pilot like his brother. His family has grown too. In addition to his wife and the three children he had in 1881 he now has five more – Ann (10), Evan (6), William (5), Phoebe (2) and Mary (1).

Finally, in 1901, 'Young' Evan Morris who is actually now 54 is still a Trinity Pilot and living in the same Pilot House – now there are only four of them. His wife Jane is with him. Of the children only Hannah and Robert are left at home, but he has been joined by a nephew John Roberts (16) who is working as a plasterer.

David and his wife Ellen have disappeared from the 1901 census; we do not know what became of them but in N° 4 Mersey Street David's daughter Elizabeth (25) has married a slate quarryman called Thomas Roberts (32) who is described as the head of the household. They have two children of their own – David aged 2 and Thomas aged 2 months, and Elizabeth is also looking after her brother Evan who is now 16 – working as a Blacksmith – and her sisters Phoebe (12) and Mary (10).

'Young' Evan's daughter Jane Watkins has moved with her mariner husband John (who is away on census night) to N°s 6 and 7 Glyn Terrace – actually just one double-fronted house – and now has a young family consisting of three sons and a daughter; Evan (10), David (9), John (6) and Ellin (6 months). She also has her 18 year old unmarried sister Mary Morris living with her.

Appendix C: AN ANNOTATED BORTH-Y-GEST BIBLIOGRAPHY

Some of the books in this list are rare and hard to find. There are a number of internet sites which often yield treasure, including Amazon.co.uk, Abebooks.co.uk and Alibris.co.uk, and you can usually find copies through our wonderful County Library Service.

The Census records from 1841 to 1911, Tithe commutation maps and many other records are available from the County Archive, Caernarfon, or over the Internet from Ancestry.com

'Atlas of Caernarvonshire' edited by T M Bassett & B L Davies. Gwynedd Rural Council 1977. ISBN 0 903935 05 8

An excellent general source, out of print but usually available on the internet.

'Eifionydd A study in Landownership from the Medieval Period to the Present Day' by Colin A Gresham. University of Wales Press 1973. ISBN: 0-7083-0435-4

Some of the maps in the previous book are reproduced from this book which is the definitive work on land ownership in Eifionydd. The book, unfortunately, is very rare and correspondingly very expensive.

'Y Gestiana' by Alltud Eifion (Robert Isaac Jones). 1892. Facsimile edition 1975 by Gwasg Tŷ ar y Graig. English translation (typescript) 1988 by J Kidd. Revised unpublished translation 2008 by Richard Walwyn

Written in Welsh, this is the only history devoted to the Township of Gest. It has a lot in it, not all of which is reliable, and it is quite confusing to read but is really essential.

'Porthmadog Ships' by Emrys Hughes and Aled Eames. Gwynedd Archives Service 1975

This is the authoritative text on the whole subject of shipping in Borth-y-Gest and Porthmadog; a must have.

'Hanes Porthmadog' by Edward Davies

Written in Welsh and largely concerned with the ecclesiastical history of Porthmadog it contains as an appendix an English transcription of the report of 1682 into the ownership of land in Gest, including Borth-y-Gest.

'Madocks & the Wonder of Wales' by Elisabeth Beazley. Faber & Faber 1967. 2nd Ed. P&Q 1985

Elisabeth Beazley was an architect and town planner of distinction. This wonderful book which is criminally out of print is by far the best source for the story of Madocks and the development of Traeth Mawr.

'Immortal Sails' by Lt.-Colonel Henry Hughes. Robert Ross & Co. undated

Henry Hughes who lived in Borth-y-Gest and sailed in local ships tells the story of Borth-y-Gest, Porthmadog and the ships – readily available.

'Porthmadog' by Myfanwy Morris. Cyngor Sir Gwynedd undated ISBN 0 901337 51 X

A very rare and correspondingly expensive collection of old photographs of the area.

'A History of Caernarvonshire 1284–1900' by A H Dodd. Caernarvonshire Historical Society 1968

A standard academic work, but still a good read.

'The Book of Harlech' by Lewis William Lloyd. Barracuda Books Ltd. 1986. ISBN 0 86023 280 8

An admirable but quite rare book which tells the story of 'the other shore'

'The Coastline of England and Wales' by J A Steers. Cambridge University Press 1946

The standard academic work on the geography of the coast; useful for reference.

'Sir John Owen, Royalist Major-General' by Norman Tucker

This gives a full account of the larger than life Sir John Owen of Clenennau and his exploits in the Civil War.

'Clenennau Letters and Papers in the Brogyntyn Collection' T. Jones Pierce (Ed.) National Library of Wales 1947

The letters, dating from 1584 to 1620, written to William Maurice of Clenennau and collected in the Brogyntyn Archive in the National Library of Wales have been calendared (dated and summarised). They give a vivid picture of life in the area during the time of the Spanish Armada and later.

'An Inventory of the Ancient Monuments in Caernarvonshire volume II: Central' RCHAMW 1960

The Royal Commission on Ancient and Historical Monuments in Wales carried out an authoritative survey of the ancient monuments in Caernarfonshire published in 1960. Full of information it includes maps and plans of local features and houses.

'North Wales delineated from two excursions through all the interesting parts etc.' by Rev. W. Bingley ISBN:1-900941-13-9

In 1798 and 1804 the Rev Bingley toured North Wales and published his highly entertaining accounts in 1814. They give a memorable account of conditions in our area at the end of the eighteenth century before Madocks made his mark. It was republished in facsimile by Denbighshire County Council.

'A Description of Caernarvonshire (1809-1811)' by Hall, Edmund Hyde; T. Jones Pierce and Emyr Gwynne Jones (Eds.)

Another early nineteenth century history of Caernarfonshire with lots of maps and statistics.

'The History of the Gwydir Family' by Sir John Wynn ISBN: 9781141502134

Sir John Wynn of Gwydir (1553-1627) wrote his family history in about 1620. The manuscript was first published in 1770. It gives an entertaining and informative account of the area, available as a print-on-demand reproduction over the internet.

'Sails on the Dwyryd' by M. J. T. Lewis 1989 Plas Tan y Bwlch

A marvellous book that has become quite difficult to acquire. It details the history of the Dwyryd, the river leading to Traeth Bach, and helps set the scene for the ferries travelling across the Traeth from Borth-y-Gest to Ynys.

To consult Samuel Lewis's *'A Topographical Dictionary of Wales'* the easiest way is to see the version wonderfully available in the British History Online website.

Appendix D: EXTRACTS AND ARTICLES

Here are reproduced a small collection of pieces reproduced because they throw interesting light on the history of Borth-y-Gest which may be hard to find; the first is a description of the parish of Ynyscynhaearn (in which Borth-y-Gest stood) published in 1833.

1. Ynyscynhaearn from '*A Topographical Dictionary of Wales*' by Samuel Lewis, 1833

"*YNYSCYNHAIARN (YNYS-CYNHAIARN), a parish, comprising the town of Tremadoc (which is described under its own head), in the hundred of EIVIONYDD, county of CARNARVON; NORTH WALES, and containing 1075 inhabitants. This parish, which derives its name from its low maritime situation, and the dedication of its church to St. Cynhaiarn, who flourished about the close of the sixth century, is situated o n the Traeth Mawr, and on the turnpike road from Pwllheli to Tremadoc. The surface is very uneven, and in some parts mountainous; and the soil varies exceedingly, but in the lower grounds is fertile. In the mountainous parts copper-ore is found in various places, but none of the mines are worked with spirit or success. The living is annexed to the rectory of Criccieth, in the archdeaconry of Merioneth, and diocese of Bangor. The church is now being rebuilt upon a more commodious site, in the later style of English architecture, and, when completed, will be a very handsome structure: the churchyard has been very considerably enlarged; a measure rendered absolutely necessary from the increase of population which has taken place since the formation of the town and port of Tremadoc. There are places of worship for Independents and Calvinistic and Wesleyan Methodists. The poor children of this parish are entitled to the benefit of gratuitous instruction in the school at Criccieth. The average annual expenditure for the relief of the poor of the whole parish amounts to £329.7.*"

2. Terrier of Ynys Cynhaearn Church' from '*Y Gestiana*'
The next is reproduced from '*Y Gestiana*' by Robert Isaac Jones (Alltud Eifion). A terrier was a formal statement of the property and income of a parish. This terrier was of the parish of Ynyscynhaearn in 1874, but it clearly relates to an earlier age because tithes were commuted to cash in the 1840s.

Terrier Of Ynys Cynhaiarn Church
"*A true and perfect Account and Terrier of all Tithes, Pensions, Profits, Rights, Goods and implements, belonging to the Rectory, Parish and Parish Church of Ynys Cynhaiarn in the County of Carnarvon and the Diocese of Bangor, taken, made and renewed 10th day December 1784 and exhibited before the Worshipful Thomas Beven, Doctor of Laws, Chancellor of the aforesaid Diocese, at the primary Visitation of the Right Reverend Father in God, John, Lord Bishop of Bangor held at Bangor aforesaid, the 14th day of September in the year aforesaid.*

"There are belonging to the Rector, First a Modus of 2 pence for each farm in lieu of Tythe Hay, also the Tythe of all Corn in kind, also the Tythe of Wool, being the tenth part, and three half pence for each Wether sold unsheared. Also the Tythe of Lambs in their proper kind and the custom concerning them is this: if a person's number is one he pays 3d, if two 6d, if four 12d, if five 15d, if six 18d, if seven he pays a lamb, the Rector paying back 9d, if 8 – 6d, if 9 – 3d, if 10 the Rector hath the lamb complete. And in like manner for every number above 10, and every lamb sold before the time of Tything – 3d, the usual time of Tything is some few days before the first day of July being Criccieth Fair Day. The lambs are all turned together, the owner takes his choice Lamb and his choice Ewe Lamb then the Rector takes his choice Lamb, and so on alternately until the Rector hath his number. Also the Tythe of Kids and Geese, one out of three, one only out of three-score of each kind. Also the Tythe of Pigs, one out of each litter if there are three or more in the Litter. For every Mare and Colt, two pence. For every Cow and Calf, three half pence, excepting the first Calf, for which a penny is paid. The Tythe of Hemp and Honey in kind, and also Flax. For every wedding five shillings. An oblation of one shilling for every churching of women, Oblations at Funerals at Discretion. The Tythe of Eggs about Easter, two for each Cock, one for each Hen. Easter dues, sixpence for each married couple, two pence from each person of age to communicate. There is also due to the Parish Clerk a shilling for every wedding, for every Funeral oblations at discretion, there is due to him from his Rector, two pence for every churching of women, and two pence from each married couple as Easter Dues."

3. The Ferry Tragedy

In 1862 there was an accident when the ferry, by then running from Porthmadog to Ynys, capsized. This gives some idea of the conditions that might have been met by the ferry when it ran from Borth-y-Gest to Clogwyn Melyn. Those who sail on the estuary will know how quickly the weather can change, and how frightening it can be if you are trying to get back to Borth-y-Gest when a sudden gale blows up from the south west. Taken from the '*North Wales Chronicle*' (Oct 4th 1862)

Tragedy – The Sinking of the Ferry
Thursday the 7th of August 1862, one of the ferries owned by Rees Jones was returning from Porthmadog to Ynys, Talsarnau with nine passengers and two half casks of port on board. The wind had picked up and was blowing from the south west, but nobody at the time felt under any kind of

threat. About half way across, the wind freshened suddenly and created waves that made it impossible to control the vessel. In a short period of time the ferry filled with water and overturned throwing everybody overboard into the churning sea.

Another ferry was only a short distance away, sailing as quickly as they could to try and reach the stricken vessel with the hope of saving some of the passengers. The crew of the second ferry described how they could see people in the water, arms flailing and screaming for help. Only two were saved – the ferry owner and Ann Lewis, Llechwedd, Harlech. The other eight succumbed to the depths. On the Friday morning, following the tragedy seven bodies were retrieved from the beach.

An inquest was held on Monday 11th August by the coroner Griffith Williams, and Edmund Edwards acting as head juror came to the conclusion that the eight had 'drowned due to an accident'. Those that lost their lives were: John and Rees Jones, two seamen and sons to Robert Jones, Dyffryn Ardudwy; Arthur Jones the grandson of Rees Jones the ferry owner; Dorothy, the wife of Evan Lloyd, Llechwedd; Griffith a John Edwards, the sons of William Edwards, Cwrt Rasus; Ann Williams, Llanllyfni and Jane Parry, Yr Ynys whose body was never found.

Later another story from the *'North Wales Chronicle'* tells of the discovery of the missing body:

BODY FOUND. – Our readers will remember the awful catastrophe which a few weeks ago occurred at the Portmadoc Ferry, by which eight persons were at once swept into eternity without thought or preparation. All the bodies were recovered at the time except one, viz, that of Jane Parry, a milliner, who lived at Tŷ Gwyn, on the Merionethshire side of the river. The case of this poor girl was sad and melancholy in the extreme. She was the chief support of her widowed mother, and was greatly respected by every one as a prudent and good young woman. She was about being married to a captain, and her journey to Portmadoc was on purpose to purchase her wedding dress, etc. On Friday morning last, an old man named Griffith Morris, a small farmer living at Morfa Bychan, was collecting sea-weed on the shore there, when he found the body of the deceased lying on the beach, and as it would seem he recognised her. He then lifted the corpse into the cart, and proceeded at once to Portmadoc and informed the police of the circumstances. Numbers of people crowded round the cart and much sorrow was felt by all at such an untimely end. The body was then taken to Ynyscynhaiarn Parish Church, there to await the coroner's inquest, before H. Hunter Hughes, Esq., which took place on Saturday last, when a verdict of "Found drowned" was returned.

4. The Pilots' Accident

In 1880 there was a tragic accident which led to the deaths of four of Borth-y-Gest's eight pilots. The account is reproduced from the '*Carnarvon and Denbigh Herald*', for Saturday April 24th 1880

Sad Fatality at Porthmadog – Three Pilots Drowned
A few weeks back I observed that the neighbourhood had become notorious for the frequency of accidents and other extraordinary incidents. This week again I have to record one of the saddest that ever took place here, through which three persons lost their lives.

About ten-o-clock last Friday, a boat started from Borth, containing five pilots viz John Richards, John Williams (Nº 1 as he was called), John Jones, Richard Williams and Evan Morris, with the object of meeting a ship supposed to be in the bay. After crossing the Bar, it was understood that there was no ship; but as the steamer Rebecca, which had reached the Bar, was in need of a pilot, John Richards was taken on board of her. The tug-boat (Captain Rees Jones) was also out. Instead of going on board the tug-boat or the Rebecca, the four pilots, John Jones, John Williams, Richard Williams, and Evan Morris, sailed home in the boat.

There was a considerable sea on the Bar; the wind blew stiffly and the weather was uncommonly cold. In about quarter of an hour after placing John Richards on board the Rebecca, a sea swept over a part of the hinder part of the boat (which was sailing before the wind), and it was immediately filled. Having recovered themselves, the pilots decided on keeping to their boat, come what might. John Williams secured himself at the stern of the boat; John Jones by grasping the seat nearest to him; Richard Williams by tying his arms around the mast and a part of the seat and Evan Morris by placing his foot under the hole of the scuttle. While in these positions another sea came and, by lifting up one side of the boat, hurled the unfortunate men into the sea. They had a fearful battle with the elements. By heroism and determination they all succeeded in getting into the boat again, excepting poor John Jones. He was seen drowning close to them in the midst of the raging waves. Evan Morris, being a powerful young man, told Richard Williams and John Williams to keep their courage – that they would shortly reach the land. While the latter two were clinging to the seats in the boat, Evan Morris struggled with the mast that had got loose, to keep the boat from capsizing face downwards. But alas! another tremendous wave rushed and hurled them all into the sea. Richard Williams was lost this time. By extraordinary efforts, John Williams and Evan Morris succeeded in once more boarding the boat, and there the former complained that he could no longer hold on, and John Williams was swept overboard into a watery grave. By this time there was only Evan Morris left. He did all he could to keep himself in the boat until he reached the breakers, where he feared he would be killed. Trusting to the loosed mast, and divesting himself of his upper clothes, he supported himself on the mast, bravely fighting the furious waves. Being tired of supporting himself on the mast, he decided on placing it between his legs, paddling with his hands. While in that awful position he found that he was nearing Graig Ddu. He felt the cramp coming upon him, and he was also suffering intensely from the cold. After the sea had frequently rushed over him he at length could feel the sand under his feet and, in his joy, he let go the mast. He very nearly lost the battle through this, but fortunately was able to swim forward through the wild breakers until he safely reached the shore. Directly he was on terra firma he felt as if about to lose his senses, and began to shiver violently. A crowd of people hurried towards him and he was raised and carried to Trip farm, where he was attended to by Dr Jones-Morris. He had been in the water for about two hours. He was sufficiently recovered to go home to Borth at half past three o'clock, where there was great joy at his deliverance from what appeared to be certain death.

Between seven and eight o'clock the bodies of John Jones and John Williams were washed ashore and taken to their respective homes. Up to the hour of writing the body of Richard Williams had not been found. John Jones and John Williams were widowers, the former seventy-two and the latter forty-four years of age. I believe that Richard Williams was about forty-four. He has left a wife and four children. The boat came ashore near Graig Ddu. The general opinion is that it was a great recklessness on the part of the pilots to venture in the boat instead of going on board one of the steamers.

From '*Carnarvon and Denbigh Herald*', 24/4/1880
Inquest on the Bodies
On Monday evening an inquest was held in the schoolroom under the Independent Chapel, Borth, before Dr. Hunter Hughes and a jury of whom

Mr. John Owen, Borth Farm, was the foreman. Mr E Breese was present during the proceedings.

Evan Morris said: "I am a pilot stationed at Borth-y-Gest. Early on the morning of Friday we heard that a vessel was out in the bay. No one belonging to the tug-boat being out on the bank looking out for vessels, we went down to Portmadoc in a boat to appraise Capt Jones of the tug-boat of the fact. There were in the boat John Jones, Richard Williams, John Williams, John Richards and myself. From Portmadoc we went in the tug-boat over the bay, the boat towing behind. After going out we could not see any vessel in the bay, only the trader Rebecca (s.s), which was flying the 'Jack'. We went into the boat, steering for Rebecca, on board which we put John Richards. John Williams and myself wanted to go in the tug-boat because we were afraid of crossing the Bar in the boat, but John Jones and Richard Williams preferred to sail in the boat home, and they had their way. "The weather was too rough in my opinion. John Richards advised us also to go in the tug-boat.

"When we had gone about five minutes from the Rebecca a heavy sea came on and I put the stern of the boat to it. The sea did not come in then, but another wave almost capsized the boat, and I jumped on the keel and prevented it turning over. When it was righted I went into it again. John Jones was holding on to the mast. The boat was filled with water. The mast was knocked up through the arms of John Jones, and I saw the latter floating over the rail of the boat, his face black and foaming at the mouth. He was drowned before he was carried away. John Williams had fastened his legs round the last toft of the boat. I told him John Jones had gone. He said that he and I would soon go too, but I encouraged him to hold on, saying that I could see the James Conley in Pwll-Glan-y Môr, and I could hear the Rebecca whistling. Richard Williams was in the fore part of the boat. I was in the boat when it went on its side. Then we were all thrown out. I got into the boat again. I saw John Williams some distance from me floating, and ultimately I saw him drowning. I could render no assistance to him; it was all I could do to save myself. I did not see Richard Williams after we were washed away. The tide was in. The boat did not touch the ground. If it had I would have left immediately. I stuck to the boat all the time, and sat in its stern till I was washed overboard. I had the mast with me in the water, helping me to swim. Cramp had affected my legs. We were all certified pilots. John Jones had been a pilot for 32 years, Richard Williams about 8 years and John Williams over 40 years. John Williams was 71 years old, John Jones 70, Richard Williams 34 and myself 33. The

boat was an open one, twenty-two feet long (overall), 7 feet beam, and two feet six inches depth. There was no ballast in it, nor watertight compartments. It had a lug sail and one mast, and was a clever boat. There are none better in Carnarvonshire. It was built five years ago at Criccieth by John Edwards, who is deemed a good builder. It had been oftener in use, in all weather than the other boats. We have often been out in it before but not in it coming homeward is such weather as on this occasion. There are heavy breakers on the Bar. We had no life-buoys, nor had we any life-saving apparatus in the boat. The boat belonged to us as pilots; it was private property. There were eight of us altogether. We do not get anything from the Trinity Board. We pay six pence annually for every pound we receive to that board. The local commissioners appointed us to be pilots. The commissioners are Messrs Seymour Graves, Osmond Williams and D Homfray. The bodies I saw were those of John Jones and John Williams."

Mr Breese: "Would the boats be safer if they had watertight bulkheads fore and aft?"

Witness said the boat could not be well managed with them, as they would fill the stern and bows. Air pipes round the sides and under the tofts would be better. The coroner summed up and the jury brought in a verdict of 'Accidentally Drowned' adding, as a recommendation, that the pilot boats should have air pipes, as suggested by Evan Morris.

The view across the Traeth where the ferries once plied their trade